Educational Television

Educational Television

GEORGE N. GORDON

Associate Professor
Department of Communications
in Education
New York University

The Center for Applied Research in Education, Inc.
New York

Foreword

The status of educational television, which George Gordon describes in this book, is a result of a thirty years' struggle which has not yet been adequately chronicled.

For instance, in his presentation to the Federal Communications Commission on October 17, 1934, William S. Paley, then president of the Columbia Broadcasting System, opposed very firmly the allocation of frequencies to radio for education: "I do not believe any such realignment of existing facilities, as has been proposed, would result in a more effective service. . . ." He noted that the Columbia Broadcasting System was at that time devoting only 31 per cent of its time to commercial programs, leaving 69 per cent for education and public service. This record, he said, "acts as an important assurance that the extensive periods we are now devoting to educational, cultural, and informative programs generally, will not be shortened, even if the time comes when we sell more than 30 or 31 per cent of our hours to commercial sponsors." How valid that assurance, which effectively helped to block educational reservations, turned out to be, readers may decide for themselves. With regard to the need for the special reservation of frequencies for education, Mr. Paley asked: "Would that not constitute a needless duplication of facilities, at a needless cost to taxpayers?"

The position of the National Association of Broadcasters, and of the other networks was essentially the same as Mr. Paley's. The Columbia Broadcasting System was neither better nor worse in its position than other spokesmen for the industry.

In television, the record—with the exception of a few generous individual broadcasters—was essentially the same. The trade association did not think it was in the public interest to allocate frequencies to television for education, its numerous spokesmen reiterated. The principal trade publications and networks (especially when an allocation for education in a given area conflicted with a frequency they wanted), opposed educational television, though by now less directly and openly. One trade publication continued to call for withdrawal of educational television reservations, as a wasted resource, for years after they were made.

In Illinois, the state broadcasters' association, through a willing citizen, filed a taxpayer suit to prevent the State University from having its own educational television station. A widely distributed pamphlet asked: "Do we want a giant TV propaganda mill owned and controlled by [the] nation's educators?"

The pioneers who fought education's battle, though idealistic dreamers, were a hardy breed. Vilification saddened them and slowed them down and toughened them—but it did not stop them. Many of the scars from those days are not visible to outsiders. They are not entirely forgotten by some members of that old generation, like the present writer, who rub them thoughtfully from time to time even today.

Now that educational television is a reality, the atmosphere is better and friendlier. People who favor educational television are no longer radicals; they are accepted in the best of circles.

Not entirely, however. For, having noted that effective teaching is indeed possible via the medium of television, educators are likely to begin to ask troublesome questions.

If we now know how much and how irresistibly television teaches, how can it be said that we don't have any "solid evidence" that people may also be learning how to solve problems by violence and other such means in view of the "lessons" broadcast daily and nightly? If television is so effective in teaching, how can it be so in- effective in teaching the violence and other anti-social behavior it so often shows?

How are children—who have so far been taught and trained by the commercial medium itself to expect television to be *entertain- ing*—how are these children to be re-educated to be willing to use it for *hard* or critical instead of *soft* uses? And how are the be- havior patterns and language problems (Johnny can't read or write) related to television? How does one handle problems which result from "salesman grammar" ("Winstons taste good, like . . .")? How are such "lessons" to be untaught, when students protest to an- guished and impatient teachers: "But I heard it on television"?

There is then yet a danger that educators may concentrate on educational television so much that they neglect their citizen responsibilities regarding the commercial use of the medium. No matter how clean one's yard may be, if one is surrounded by acres of weeds, which seeds will be blown over?

I would urge that in their preoccupation with education's own stations, readers not forget that commercial broadcasters are still licensed to operate in the broad public interest. This includes the promotion of education and educational values and even the development of intellectuals, troublesome as many broadcasters may find the latter.

This book does provide a useful perspective for the understanding of educational television. But it should also do more than this. It is to be hoped that some of the principles and lessons growing out of educational uses, which Dr. Gordon reports, may find wider application and provoke more useful discussion.

HARRY J. SKORNIA
Professor of Radio and Television
College of Journalism and Communications
University of Illinois

Educational Television

George N. Gordon

In a period of American education marked by numerous innovations, educational television stands out as the most comprehensive and dramatic of the new media. Its educational value is, however, quite controversial. This book makes a thorough presentation of educational television and provides the evidence by which the reader can resolve, in his own mind, the conflicting claims made by its supporters and critics.

Educational Television is, in one sense, a primer in that it contains definitions and explanations of terms and concepts. The difference between closed-circuit and open-circuit television, for instance, is explained in a nontechnical yet complete and understandable manner. The book is technically accurate without lapsing into jargon.

The history of educational television, financial bases, the public service aspects, the effects of educational and instructional television, and the future of both, constitute the content of the book. The relevant research is brought to bear on all issues in a skillful manner. All of the significant experiments in educational television are presented and discussed. The reader can judge the value of the medium as it is used in Washington County, Maryland, or on Sunrise Semester, or on MPATI. The book contains numerous examples and illustrations of educational and instructional television.

Dr. George N. Gordon is an Associate Professor of Communications in Education in the School of Education, New York University. He is the author of books and articles on educational television as well as other aspects of communications.

DANIEL E. GRIFFITHS
Content Editor

Contents

CHAPTER I

A Story of Educational Broadcasting   1

     Introduction   1
     The Growth of Educational Television   4
     Educational Television Abroad   14

CHAPTER II

The Financing of Educational Television   17

     Cost of Educational Television   18
     Financing for the Future   22

CHAPTER III

Educational Television and Public-Service
     Broadcasting   29

     Commercial Channels   30
     Educational Channels   33
     Networks and Program Content   34
     Criticisms of Public-Service Broadcasting   36

CHAPTER IV

The Effects of Public-Service Television   39

   Broadcasts on Commercial Channels   39

   Broadcasts on Educational Stations   41

   *Competition Between Commercial and Educational
      Stations*   44

   Audiences for Educational Broadcasts   46

CHAPTER V

Instructional Television in the United States   51

   On Commercial Stations   51

   On Educational Stations   53

   On Closed-Circuit Installations   57

   Production Facilities   60

   Message Transmission   63

CHAPTER VI

Instructional Television in Schooling   65

   The Uses of Instructional Television   66

   Teaching by Television   67

   Television in the Classroom   70

   Using Instructional Television   73

   Articulation of Instruction   78

CHAPTER VII

Effectiveness of Instructional Television 83

Matched-Group Experiments 83

Attitudes Toward Instructional Television 90

CHAPTER VIII

The Future of Instructional Television 97

Open-Circuit Television 98

Closed-Circuit Television 100

Bibliography 107

Index 109

CHAPTER I

A Survey of Educational Broadcasting

Introduction

"The best education," A. N. Whitehead stated in the second decade of this century, "is to be found in gaining the utmost information from the simplest apparatus."

The advances made in technology since Whitehead's advice was first published have in no manner diminished its relevance to education. Simplicity remains the main key to effective teaching and efficient learning on all levels of education. Neither advances in educational theory nor innovations in instructional methods have altered the axiom that what is taught and learned best, under most circumstances, is that which has been broken down into its simplest elements and projected to the student in its least involved form. Even the complex psychological theories underlying programmed instruction, which has spawned the mechanical and electronic teaching machinery on the market today, are attempts to reduce complicated ideas to their least involved—and, therefore, most easily learned—components.

What *has* changed in this era of population explosions and technological revolutions is the very meaning of the word *education,* which today must be taken to mean *free universal education,* a phrase that is less a description than a fundamental mandate for action in almost every nation in the modern world. "The best education," as Whitehead put it, may still rely on an appreciation of the virtues of simplicity; but the problem of transmitting education of any sort to the more than 40 million Americans in the country's various schools today—to say nothing of the countless millions of other people of all ages who are slaking their thirst for schooling abroad—is another matter. For many educators it remains an issue so complicated that they prefer to cultivate their own parts of the pedagogical garden in the hope that it will go away or, somehow, resolve itself.

1

Problems of enormous size and complexity, however, face educators and laymen almost everywhere on the globe. Numerous plans for elementary, secondary, and higher education, conceived with ingenuity and foresight, have been proposed in America and elsewhere. Many of these schemes include various uses of television. In fact, television has frequently been discussed by educators as one of the *simplest* means of unraveling the knotty quantitative academic and administrative difficulties that face the world.

This book will attempt, with a minimum of special interest or partisan zeal on a subject which lacks neither, to offer the reader a broad view of many of these plans, to explain their technical and administrative aspects, and to clarify the relevance of the medium of television to the goals of education at all levels.

Definitions

Educational television. The first obstacle on the path of simplicity is the problem of terminology. Popular usage has permitted the term *educational television* to cover almost any sort of educational video program presented for any serious purpose or in an attempt to teach something to someone. This broad definition of the term will be maintained throughout this book. But because it is such a general term, which may include so many types of electronic transmission of such different material, it will always be qualified to indicate: (1) what kind of education is being broadcast, (2) to whom, (3) for what reason, and (4) how (or by what kind of electronic transmission). These same qualifications will also refer to the phrase *educational broadcasting,* which also includes radio transmission.

The following terms are commonly used by many—but not all— educational broadcasters in the United States:

Instructional television. The term *instructional television* will be used to refer to electronic transmissions whose function is to teach a specific body of subject matter to students at home or in school, when this subject matter is part of a formal course of study. Instructional television may be transmitted in any number of ways. The method of broadcasting is irrelevant to its purpose. Programs of instructional television may or may not be conducted by teachers. At present, they usually are, but it is quite possible for an instructional television program to be produced without a conventional teacher or a professional actor playing the part of teacher, and even without a narrator or announcer of any sort. An historical pageant, for instance, presented as part of a history course, would constitute an instructional television program.

Closed-circuit broadcasting. Broadcasts transmitted to a definitely prescribed area, in such a manner that conventional receiving sets cannot pick them up, are called *closed-circuit broadcasts.* Closed-circuit systems usually transmit by means of coaxial cables or low-powered broadcasts (or the picture may be sent by coaxial cable and the sound by a separate circuit). There is no reason, however, why closed-circuit broadcasts cannot be sent through the air (by microwave relay) over a frequency which cannot be picked up by conventional receivers tuned only for commercial frequencies, or by "scrambled signals," which can be unscrambled only on sets electronically modified to receive them.

Open-circuit broadcasts. Conventional broadcasts, transmitted over one or more of the frequencies assigned to a given area, are called *open-circuit broadcasts.* Standard television receivers can usually tune in these broadcasts. The range of open-circuit transmission covers a radius of about fifty miles (more or less, depending on power, geographical contours, and other factors). The signal must be amplified or rebroadcast if it is to be received in areas beyond this radius.

VHF and UHF bands. At present, most open-circuit broadcasting is transmitted on VHF (Very High Frequency) bands, which permits a total of seven stations to broadcast at the same time without interference. But more than ten years after these VHF frequencies had first been assigned, another set of seventy UHF (Ultra-High Frequency) channels were found to be feasible. Throughout the United States, however, most television broadcasting today is still transmitted on the scarce VHF bands, because most receivers are not equipped for UHF signals. To equip them would require adapters costing from five to fifty dollars. Some commercial broadcasts, as well as some educational ones, are carried by UHF frequencies in areas where the purchase of adapters has been heavy or where all transmissions are made on UHF bands. A recent ruling by the Federal Communications Commission (FCC) has made it mandatory that all receivers manufactured after April 30, 1964 must be capable of receiving UHF signals in preparation for the

not-too-distant day when all open-circuit broadcasting in the United
States will be shifted to these frequencies.

These, then, are the main terms used to describe educational television in the pages that follow. Other specialized words will be described in the text as this new medium of communication and instruction is examined.

One concluding point: in its own way, educational television may
become as important to education as the invention of movable type
was to the mass production of books. Television is capable of making a considerable contribution to the solution of many teaching
and learning problems. Although it may not revolutionize our concepts of schooling or the values of education, it will play a formative
role in institutions of learning, high and low, in the very near future.

The Growth of Educational Television

From the first days of radio broadcasting, in the early twentieth
century, pioneers in radio recognized that this medium, with its
capacity for reaching a great number of homes simultaneously,
must have some sort of educational value. They were eager to see
this new force used for the common good—to lift the general cultural tone of the nation. Some published statements to this effect[1]
and, during this period of radio's infancy, institutions of higher
education were among the most frequent applicants for licenses to
broadcast. These first college stations did not last long, however,
for the commercial nature and direction of radio broadcasting in
the United States was clarified during the early 1920's. The educators could not compete with commercial radio.

With the establishment of the FCC in 1934, however, attention
once again turned the possible uses of radio as a medium of instruction. But the proponents of educational broadcasting, in Congress and elsewhere, eventually yielded to commercial interest; by
1936, the issue was all but closed once more. A handful of educational programs were offered by the major networks as part of
their obeisance to the nonprofit "public service" aspect of broadcasting. A few municipally sponsored stations came into existence
and several colleges or universities operated stations as an extracur-

---

[1] Sidney W. Head, *Broadcasting in America* (Boston: Houghton Mifflin Company, 1956), pp. 105–106.

ricular activity for those students who were interested in broadcasting as a career.

The history of television has been told so many times that it is, by now, almost a part of the national folklore: Zworkykin's experiments during the 1920's; RCA's early interest in the technology of video and leadership by the BBC in Britain during the 1930's; and, finally, the first public television broadcasts of the opening of the New York World's Fair in 1939 over NBC's experimental station W2XBS.

The unbelievably rapid development of television as an instrument of mass communication has become a cliché testament both to technological advance and to the avidity with which new things are grasped and taken for granted by the public. So great and so fast has been this growth that any thumbnail sketch is out of date by the time it is printed.

The year 1948 marked the start of television's ascendancy in America: network broadcasts had begun at the end of World War II, the production of receivers soared, and advertising support—so vital to commercial broadcasting—began to switch from other media to television.

At present, about 50 million (maybe 60 million by the time you read this) American homes have one or more television sets. The average receiver is turned on about six hours a day. At least 70 million Americans watched the first debate between Presidential candidates Kennedy and Nixon in 1960; and, it is estimated, as many as 100 million people watched various parts of the three-day video coverage of the events following the assassination of President Kennedy in November 1963.[2]

The meaning of these figures is enhanced by comparable statistics for other mass media in the United States: the number of newspapers circulated daily (about 60 million), weekly attendance at the movies during a good week at the nation's box offices (about 40 million), or the combined subscription statistics per issue for *The Reader's Digest, Life* and *Look* (about 27 million). From television-viewing statistics may also be extrapolated sundry startling assertions: for instance, it is claimed that the audience for *a single performance* of *Oedipus Rex* (presented on the *Omnibus* tele-

---

[2] Columbia Broadcasting System, *Newsletter* (December 12, 1963), 18–19.

vision program some years ago) *was larger than all the audiences combined at all the performances since the fifth century* B.C. Such comparisons prove that a lot of people watch television or, put another way, that television has the capacity for reaching vast numbers of people.

The formative period. Although radio's contribution to American education may be little noted nor long remembered, its potential as an instrument of enlightenment has not gone unnoticed. Even with the end of its great period as a major commercial medium, communications experts still foresee a productive future for educational sound broadcasting. Their arguments are convincing, particularly when they cite the record of the BBC's school broadcasts and adult education programs, used by thousands of schools in Great Britain. These programs are also accompanied by text materials of first-rate aesthetic, as well as educational, quality.[3]

In the United States, however, considerable effort was expended to introduce radio broadcasting to the task of education. Between 1920 and 1930, between 176 and 200 schools, colleges, and universities constructed radio stations. Because of the Great Depression and because educational broadcasting did not live up to its early expectations, a mere thirty-five were still in operation by the end of the 1930's, most of them used for extension education in land-grant colleges.

Educational broadcasting through this period was sustained, in part, by such institutions as the National Association of Educational Broadcasters, Ohio State University's annual International Institute for Education by Radio, and other visionary groups around the country. With their help—and an occasional assist from commercial broadcasters via programs like the weekly *School of the Air* and *The Town Meeting of the Air,* programs on municipal stations, and the like—educational radio limped along into the 1940's.[4]

At the end of World War II, FM (Frequency Modulation) broadcasting was introduced, and with it came a new spectrum of stations. They gave radio its second chance, as Charles Siepmann

---

[3] Charles A. Siepmann, *Radio, Television, and Society* (New York: Oxford University Press, Inc., 1950), pp. 252–91.

[4] Richard B. Hull, "A Note on the History of ETV" in *Educational Television: The Next Ten Years* (Stanford: The Institute for Communication Research, 1962), pp. 337–39.

said in his angry but provocative book.[5] Siepmann's vision included an alternate, semieducational, national FM radio service, serving the listening needs of minority groups from coast to coast. What Siepmann could not foresee, however, was the rise of television during the late 1940's and the fact that, by 1948, radio would be—for educational purposes at least—a moribund medium.

The potential uses of radio for schooling, therefore, remain largely unexploited. The arrival of television further eclipsed the possibilities for the use of radio instruction on any level of education. Now pictures, black and white or in color, have added to the possibilities of sound broadcasting and, beside television, radio seems like child's play. After World War II, television, with what many believed was far greater potential for use in schooling, took center stage as *the* new educational medium. In educational circles other audiovisual media—motion pictures, tape recordings, records, filmstrips, and slides—paled in comparison. During the next ten or more years (1950–60), television received the lion's share of the support given, by the largest educational foundations and by the government, to encourage development of new teaching techniques. "Teach by television!" became the new educational battle-cry, sometimes (in the opinion of many) hurled in defiance of logic, both by professional educators and by public figures. By 1963, the role of television in education had changed, assuming a less dominant position among other new teaching and learning devices, but finding for itself a permanent place in American educational life.

Open-circuit educational television. By 1948, the postwar boom in the manufacture of television receiving sets and demands for broadcasting licenses had placed inordinate pressure upon the FCC, whose responsibility it was to see that these franchises were distributed equitably and in the best public interest. Under pressure of many kinds, the FCC held a number of hearings on the problem of station allocation. Among spokesmen for other interests, distinguished educators and representatives of groups of educational broadcasters voiced their hope that certain frequencies would be reserved for educational use rather than for commercial purposes. At that time, every station then in operation was commercially fi-

---

[5] Charles A. Siepmann, *Radio's Second Chance* (Boston: Little, Brown & Co., 1946).

nanced, and it looked as if no specific allocations might be made for educational television of any sort.

It was not until three years later, in 1951, that the FCC finally took specific notice of the need for educational television open-circuit stations in the United States. This recognition was largely the result of the consistent labors of Commissioner Freida Hennock, long one of educational broadcasting's most enthusiastic proponents. By 1952, after a "freezing" of station allocations (during which time the FCC suspended all applications for stations of any kind), 242 channels in the television spectrum were reserved for noncommercial or educational use.

Eighty of these stations were on VHF channels, while 162 were in UHF wave lengths. (This number was later raised to 89 VHF and 178 UHF allocations of the 267 channels finally reserved for educational purposes.) Although the action was taken by the FCC alone, these allocations were also partly the result of influences brought to bear upon the agency by educational broadcasters and their spokesmen from many regions of the country. These individuals enlisted the support of national educational groups and public figures of considerable prestige. Pressure and counterpressure marked the period 1951–52, at the end of which these specific allocations were finally announced. For a time it seemed as if no one could be quite entirely satisfied with the FCC's provisions for educational television, for these specifically forbid educational stations to engage in any kind of commercial activity which might help to finance them. Obviously, a new kind of funding had to be conceived.

Many observers viewed with reservations the channels finally allocated to educational purposes. While gratified at the number of channels, they voiced doubts about the overwhelming proportion of UHF allocations, as well as the geographical distribution of the stations: there were few desirable channels in large cities and certain states seemed to receive less than their due share.[6] Even with the increase in the number of channels (to 267), the over-all proportion of VHF and UHF stations remained about the same. But most educational broadcasters agreed that the allocations would

---

6 John Walker Powell, *Channels of Learning* (Washington, D.C.: Public Affairs Press, 1962), pp. 22–25.

stand more or less as granted in 1952, and that they had better make do with whatever had been reserved for them.

Having lost their chance to use radio for education, most parties interested in educational broadcasting greeted this move by the FCC with enthusiasm. Their initial burst of energy was to continue unabated and to spread to many quarters of the academic community during the next ten years.

Within a year after the allocations were made, Station KUHT, supported by the University of Houston and the Houston School District, came on the air. By 1955 nine other stations had begun transmission in Pittsburgh, Madison (Wisconsin), San Francisco, Cincinnati, St. Louis, Lincoln (Nebraska), Seattle, Manford (Alabama), and Chapel Hill (North Carolina). Between 1953 and 1957 five commercial or noneducational stations were licensed to and operated by educational institutions: Notre Dame, South Bend, (Indiana), Iowa State, Ames (Iowa), Loyola University, New Orleans, the University of Missouri, Columbia (Missouri), and St. Norbert College, Green Bay (Wisconsin). These institutions operate them both as commercial and as educational stations, offering alternate kinds of service.

During the years that followed, many other stations began operations, and, by the spring of 1964, more than ninety nonprofit educational television stations were broadcasting in the United States. The period was also marked by despair over the few available frequencies being used for educational broadcasting (out of more than 250) and by pride at those outlets which had begun to transmit educational programs. The record for this early period shows the failure of only one station: Station KTHE of Los Angeles, which was operating on a UHF channel in a community where most receivers were constructed to receive only VHF broadcasts.

The growth pattern of these stations was largely determined by financing, a complex problem treated in detail in Chapter II. It is sufficient to explain here that Philip Lewis, an expert on the cost of television broadcasting, notes that it requires somewhere between $300,000 and $500,000 to build a television station for educational broadcasting.[7] Others have placed operating budgets at

---

[7] Philip Lewis, *Educational Television Guidebook* (New York: McGraw-Hill Book Company, 1961), p. 32.

between $76,000 to about $1 million (with a median of $275,000) *per year*.[8] Large sums of money must, of course, be raised for the construction and development of educational resources of any kind, but the development of educational open-frequency broadcasting, relegated to a nonprofit status by the FCC, had to await the accumulation of considerably more capital than educators are used to spending for conventional schooling.

To describe specifically just where the money came from is difficult. Siepmann[9] cites various sources for what he calls the "first funding of this great adventure": state legislatures, universities, city governments, boards of education, commercial broadcasting outlets, private businesses, and even private citizens enthusiastic about the course (and potential effects) of educational television. All these sources were tapped at various times to pay for certain aspects of station construction and operation.

Lewis differentiates[10] between *single-agency stations,* for which one educational agency is the licensee; *community stations,* for which a nonprofit organization (such as a civic cultural group) is set up to oversee the broadcasting operation; and *state-network stations,* for which a state educational agency is the actual licensee for a number of stations in a single state (most notably in Alabama and Florida). These organizational patterns, all employed by stations now on the air, reflect great differences in the financing of station construction and operation. It is obvious that interests which put money into the construction of stations are also likely to keep a close eye on how they operate.

Various educational broadcasting agencies have contributed formidably to the growth of educational television in America, both in the matter of station construction and maintenance and in the provision of films and tapes for broadcasts. There is no way to minimize the contribution of these organizations to the growth of educational broadcasting in the United States, not only in tangible ways, but also in terms of morale-building and the dissemination of vital information.

The National Educational Television and Radio Center (NET)

8 Lyle M. Nelson, "The Financing of Educational Television" in *Educational Television, The Next Ten Years, op. cit.,* p. 167.

9 Charles Siepmann, *TV and Our School Crisis* (New York: Dodd, Mead & Co., 1958), pp. 34–35.

10 Lewis, *op. cit.,* pp. 28–29.

was and is an indispensable producer and clearinghouse for program materials of all kinds. The National Association of Educational Broadcasters has been an invaluable advisory service and
information center. The Joint Council for Educational Television
an amalgamation of seven or so educational organizations, is also
concerned with the health and welfare of educational television in
America. The council, organized in March 1951 with a grant from
the Ford Foundation, constituted a powerful pressure group in giv-
ing open-circuit educational broadcasting its first chance. There
are also various regional organizations, such as the Southern Regional Education Board, and a number of other state and local
groups. Their praises have been sung with justice by many, and the
complex story of their relationship to the rise of educational television has been told elsewhere.[11]

Attention should also be devoted to the role of the federal government, through the Educational Media Branch of the U.S. Office
of Education. In addition to issuing publication and conducting
some small projects of value to many educational broadcasters, the
U.S. Office of Education also administers Title VII of the National
Defense Education Act of 1958. Although this act has been primarily concerned with research into the effects and effectiveness of
many types of open- and closed-circuit educational television, the
money that has been provided by the federal government for these
research projects has also helped broadcasters to improve their programming and has provided the stimulus for a number of ingenious
applications of television to schooling (see Chapter VI).[12]

The single major source for financing open-circuit educational
television has unquestionably been the Ford Foundation through
its many agencies, particularly the Fund for Adult Education and
the Fund for the Advancement of Education.[13] Although other
foundations have contributed to selected educational television
products, and although private industry has been reasonably generous in encouraging educational television projects (particularly
those which demonstrate the effectiveness of a specific corporation's

---

[11] Donald G. Tarbet, *Television and Our Schools* (New York: The Ronald Press
Company, 1961), pp. 8–12 and Powell, *op. cit.*, pp. 55–108.

[12] C. Walter Stone, "TV Instruction and the Federal Government" in Lee S.
Dreyfus and Wallace M. Bradley, *Televised Instruction* (Detroit: Wayne State
Mass Communications Center, 1962), pp. 17–31.

[13] Powell, *op. cit.*, pp. 58–64.

product), it has been the Ford Foundation that has poured millions into educational television in the United States. It has not only financed station construction, it has also provided subsidies for experimental programming, for educational theorizing and research on the use of television for teaching as well as on the comparison of this medium with conventional teaching devices, and (perhaps most important), for those agencies which produce and distribute filmed television materials and coordinate educational television activities.

Some writers on educational television (including the present author) have in the past expressed trepidations about the control exercised by the Ford Foundation during these years of educational television's growth.[14] In view of the Ford Foundation's amazing financial investment in an unknown quantity, these fears may have been precipitous. On the other hand, many critics overemphasized what seemed to them to be the Foundation's doctrinaire and unhealthy approach to school problems: that is, the heavy concentration on the financial economies in televised education rather than on the use of television to improve instruction. This tendency, however, seems today to have been only a passing enthusiasm of a few Ford philanthropists, rather than the general policy of the Foundation.

At the present writing, it appears that Ford, having served its purpose in stimulating educational television for ten years, is about to withdraw much of its recent support from this enterprise. The task of financing open-circuit educational television in the future therefore remains an outstanding issue which broadcasters around the country must now face. Chapter II deals with the implications of this problem for the school system.

Whatever the future of educational television in the United States, however, the role of the Ford Foundation and many of its talented and farsighted personnel will be recorded as seminal during the first decade of growth and experiment. From a broad perspective, Ford's intimate involvement in educational television is one of many examples of the ways in which large foundations are directing their energies towards the improvement of education on all levels. Their

14 Lawrence F. Costello and George N. Gordon, *Teach with Television* (New York: Hastings House, 1961), pp. 136–40.

activities constitute a patronage hitherto unknown, extended (paradoxically) in the names of the greatest—and frequently most ruthless—captains of industry in the past.

Closed-circuit educational television. This thumbnail sketch of the growth and development of educational television must include a description of the development of various systems of closed-circuit television. It would be difficult to make a complete and accurate summary of the ways in which educators have used closed-circuit television. In the first place, almost any organization, public or private, may begin closed-circuit transmissions without permission from the FCC or any other governmental agency, provided that its signal does not cross state lines or interfere with any licensed electronic communication. Second, the term *closed-circuit television* may apply to anything from the simplest gadgets in the field of video (e.g., an industrial camera wired to a conventional television receiver in a science classroom, where television is used for magnification of experiments performed by the instructor) to elaborate studio broadcasts or even to an entire school system rivaling those of commercial stations.

Details of the operation of these systems, and the modifications made by various communities, are given in Chapter V. Lewis,[15] however, notes that closed-circuit television has been used in many ways in schools, including transmission within a single room, hookups between different rooms in the same school building, interconnecting systems between schools, and complex arrangements covering entire school districts with studio facilities or origination facilities located at a number of points along the closed circuit. At present, the more elaborate systems usually employ a circuit of coaxial cables to transmit visual image and sound or to carry the picture alone (the sound being transmitted by an accompanying intercom system).

It is difficult to make a reliable estimate of the number of such systems currently in use in the United States, for they have been installed in community centers, Army and Navy educational centers, hospitals, dental clinics, and in industrial plants, where they have been pressed into service to perform many different kinds of tasks.

---

[15] Lewis, *op. cit.*, pp. 48–68.

Certainly, there are at least 1000 such installations in service in the United States today; 400–500 of these are being used by public and private schools and colleges. Their number has been increasing rapidly of late because of a dramatic decrease in the cost of simple television transmission and distribution equipment. This is mainly the result of the introduction of Japanese instruments and electronic components and the technical perfection of relatively inexpensive television tape-recording devices.

Because most of these closed-circuit systems do not require enormous capital outlays, much unpublicized experimentation with closed-circuit broadcasting has been done by individual schools, school systems, and other organizations, paid for out of existing budgets. More elaborate facilities have been financed by the Ford Foundation, which has encouraged distinctive sorts of educational experimentation with them. Ford's role in closed-circuit transmission probably has been less prominent than its role in open-circuit educational television. Open-circuit stations require the more munificent kind of patronage that only an enormous foundation like Ford could undertake.

Educational Television Abroad

Although this summary of educational television in the United States has been necessarily brief, the worldwide picture must be drawn in even more cursory terms. There is a good deal of evidence available as to how, when, and where educational television is used abroad, who will be likely to use it, and for what purposes.[16]

Regular television service is spreading abroad in a manner roughly comparable to the way in which it mushroomed in the United States. (Again, the statistics given will be out of date by the time they are published.) The world total of receiving sets in use today hovers around the 130 million mark, and 2380 transmitters are beaming programs on every continent. In Europe alone there are 1160 transmitting stations, and live broadcasts from Moscow to London and vice versa are not uncommon.[17]

Almost everywhere television goes, it is used, in one way or an-

---

16 Henry R. Cassirer, *Television Teaching Today* (Paris: UNESCO, 1960), pp. 11–267, especially pp. 250–57.

17 UNESCO *World Communications* (New York: UNESCO, 1964), p. 34.

other, for educational purposes,[18] particularly in those nations where it is difficult to disseminate information (or propaganda) by conventional devices (that is, by building schools, training teachers, and providing teaching tools, texts and other materials).

Exactly *how* any nation employs the medium of television depends upon a number of factors, having to do with the number and geographical placement of stations, the number of sets available for individual or group viewing, the major educational needs of the people (both children or adults), the adequacy of the present educational system in any given country and the general prospects for its growth. Also significant is the nature and degree of political unrest in the nation, for a well-organized educational television system can be turned, overnight, into a device for indoctrination or an instrument of revolution or counterrevolution.

In many countries—Italy, for one—television has already proved its value for adult education, particularly in the matter of teaching illiterate adults to read and write. Storytelling hours, puppet shows, and other cultural programs for youngsters are immensely popular in the Soviet Union. France and England have found many uses for in-school broadcasts, but in these countries they are designed primarily to enrich the present curriculum offerings.

Emerging African nations are faced with a dilemma: televised primary education (the type most needed) is frequently much more expensive than conventional teaching because labor, even teaching labor, is so cheap. Yet, in these same countries, educational programs would seem more adequately to justify the investment in television stations than the dubbed-in American commercial programs (particularly Westerns) which are by far their most popular television fare.

The rise of educational television is certainly not confined to the United States or even to the Western world. It is a worldwide concomitant of the current revolution in mass communication—a revolution of global dimensions, affecting not only the Free World but nations behind the Iron Curtain as well. More significantly, it touches not only the lives of citizens of affluent nations which can afford a plethora of gadgets, but it seems also to affect deeply both the education and political indoctrination of the masses in coun-

---

[18] *Educational Broadcasting Review* (September 1962), 4–40, 58–65.

tries which have been reached by few other manifestations of modern technology. In the long run, therefore, the importance of educational television may not lie in the values and functions described in this volume but, rather, in what it may accomplish tomorrow elsewhere in the world.

CHAPTER II

The Financing of Educational Television

Because interest during the past decade has been centered on the use of television for educational purposes, a relatively small amount of attention has been devoted to what would seem to be a fundamental consideration: the financing of educational television both at the present and in the future. Speculation on teaching methods, effectiveness, morale problems, and even the psychology of televised learning has run into thousands of pages of printed, mimeographed, and typed reports, but little discussion has been devoted to a hard-core question: Who will pick up the bills for educational broadcasting?

In view of the paternal (or avuncular) role of the private foundations (see Chapter I), this over-all attitude on the part of telecasters is not surprising. For a time it looked as if "Papa would provide." Many millions of dollars (well over $85 million from the Ford Foundation alone) were poured into new educational stations in order to experiment with television as a means of instruction. These early experiments, which were almost entirely subsidized by sources outside the educational world, invariably involved the purchase of equipment and/or the conversion of classroom space or the construction of "receiving classrooms" and the installation of devices for production, transmission, and reception, as well as the payment of skilled personnel.

This well eventually ran dry, despite some continuing grants by the Ford Foundation to such organizations as the National Educational Television and Radio Center in sums as high as $6 million at one time,[1] and despite a good number of continuing government subsidies for experiments involving educational television. During the early 1960's, the question of financial support pressed harder and harder upon broadcasters and school administrators who were interested in using television. In short, they were faced with two

---

[1] *NET News* (Fall 1963), 1, 14–23.

questions: How much does it cost to install and operate open- and closed-circuit television education? Who is going to pay for it, and how?

Answers to these questions seemed infinitely more difficult to come by than solutions to the various abstruse problems concerning the pedagogical effectiveness of educational television or the psychological aspects of learning by television.

Cost of Educational Television

The financial basis upon which educational television rests today and will rest tomorrow is one of the most important matters involved in determining exactly how democracies are to meet the challenge of free universal education in the generations to come.[2]

Open-circuit television. On the basis of a 1961 study of fifty-five open-circuit educational television stations, it was concluded that the operation of an educational television station is not a simple matter from the financial point of view. To begin with, these stations represented an average capital investment of $530,000 and an average annual operating budget of $270,000.

But averages do not give a very complete picture. These fifty-five stations were capitalized by, and affiliated with, different sorts of nonprofit organizations which affected, in one way or another, the amount of capital which they might procure and spend. As far as affiliation was concerned, 36 per cent were college- or university-owned, 32 per cent were community-operated, 17 per cent were licensed to a state authority, and 15 per cent were operated by school systems.

These fifty-five stations represented a wide diversity, both in capital investment and in operating costs. But an examination of each will give some indication of how much it costs to build or maintain an open-circuit educational television station.

First, as the dollar loses its value (or as the cost of living rises),

2 The information which follows has been taken mostly from Lyle M. Nelson, "The Financing of Educational Television," in *Educational Television: The Next Ten Years* (Stanford: The Institution for Communication Research, 1962), pp. 166–83. No individual page citations will be given for the material presented or the estimates made by Mr. Nelson. This article is unusual in the literature of educational television because it deals in specifics as to ongoing costs of operations and realistic predictions concerning the future of them. Mr. Nelson is presently Director of University Relations at Stanford University.

electronic equipment rises in cost. This tendency is frequently neutralized or reversed, however, by technological invention which reduces the cost of specific items. For instance, the cheapest of television-tape recorders cost over $40,000 in 1961, but these were superseded in 1963 by a model costing a quarter of that amount. Second, operating costs tend to vary, too, depending on whether skilled engineers or engineering students are employed and whether union help must be employed. These matters, like the variable cost of electricity in different parts of the country, qualify any figures projected for costs of open-circuit stations.

Of the community-operated stations, capital investments ran from $153,000 to $1.358 million, while operating budgets varied from $76,000 to $1.01 million. College or university stations showed variations from $268,500 to $980,000 on capital investments, and $50,000[3] to $569,000 on operating costs. Those stations operated by school systems showed differences of from $153,000 to $800,000 on investments, and from $122,000 to $553,000 on operating expenses. The last group in the sample, stations operated by state authorities, were capitalized at from $529,000 to $900,000 and operated on budgets of from $80,000 to $842,900.

Two main facts emerge from these survey figures. First, the "lows" for capital investment and yearly operating costs ($153,000 and $50,000, respectively) are formidable sums of money as educators reckon funds and apportion their budgets. Second, there seems to be almost no ceiling on the amount of money which may be spent in either category for open-circuit transmission. An educational station in a large city may be "worth" in excess of $6 million (or so Jack Gould reported in *The New York Times* about New York's Channel 13[4]), and such a station may cost more than $1 million a year to operate. On the other hand, it may be possible to put a low-cost UHF station on the air for as little as $50,000 and operate it for less than $35,000 per year, but such an operation, although it might deal in excellent and inventive educational programs, would be a venture in which many financial corners had been sharply cut.

---

[3] The lowest operating costs noted, probably because student personnel was employed for skilled labor.

[4] *The New York Times* (February 26, 1961).

The distribution of these sums depends, of course, upon many factors. Most important, any sums of money projected for salaries of skilled personnel—which may run from $92,000 per year for a modest VHF or UHF educational television station to about $300,000 per year at a more elaborate installation—are contingent upon a number of factors, including the amount of nonprofessional help available to man the station, the objectives of programming, and the all-important question, of whether union or nonunion labor will be used for operation. In and near big cities, it is usually mandatory to employ union personnel for technical and, sometimes, professional positions. In rural areas, this is frequently not the case, and the difference is certainly reflected in the station's budget.

On the minimum side, "average" capital cost for a satisfactory open-circuit station transmitting to a radius of ten miles or so, using two cameras, a film chain and allied equipment, and having its own transmitter, tower, antenna, and transmission lines, is about $275,000 at present. "Average" operating costs for such a station are about $30,000 per year. And as indicated above, personnel requirements will add another $92,000 or so.

On the other hand, a thoroughly professional station at today's prices, will be much more costly to build and operate. Capital costs may run to $1.3 million; operating costs, to $100,000 per year; and personnel requirements, to as much as $300,000 annually. Although such an elaborate station may be used for any educational task—for instructional broadcasting and public-service programming of every conceivable variety—costs here are comparable to commercial operations, in which the high investment is justified by the expectation of equally high profits from the sale of advertising, a practice strictly forbidden in the FCC's license provisions for educational stations.

Closed-circuit television. Experience with closed-circuit television has shown that its costs range even more widely than those for open-circuit installations. This is because the "low-budget" end of the scale can involve equipment costing a few thousand dollars, and because certain schools and school systems can cut labor costs down to almost nothing by employing amateurs and students to operate simple equipment—tasks which, in open-circuit stations, require highly specialized personnel.

A closed-circuit installation can vary from a single industrial-type camera connected to one or more nearby receivers to a complex studio with transmission and reception equipment covering numerous schoolhouses throughout an entire school district, a set-up every bit as elaborate and expensive as a professional open-circuit broadcasting system. Closed-circuit transmission need not be inexpensive or jerry-built in any way; the term does not refer to the complexity of origination or the quality of television production involved.

On the basis of 133 representative closed-circuit systems examined by Nelson,[5] it is possible to make certain generalizations about the current costs of educational television by closed-circuit transmission in the United States. They do not represent what might possibly be the upper or lower limits of expense for capital outlays or for running costs but, rather, what presently seems to be customary in the construction and operation costs of closed-circuit installations.

Whether the picture will change in the future depends upon the new and possibly unforeseen uses which educators may find for closed-circuit television as a means of communication within and among school buildings, and on the future costs of equipment. These costs seem, at present, to be decreasing because of the use of simplified electronic devices, such as printed circuits, and as a result of the importation of Japanese components and equipment, which are frequently noticeably cheaper than their American counterparts and no less effective.

Realistic closed-circuit capital outlay probably starts at the low figure of $8000 and runs as high as $250,000—a sum comparable to the price of installing an open-circuit station. Maintenance costs may differ as widely: from $6000 to as much as $215,000 per year.

A satisfactory closed-circuit television system, using professional cameras, a film chain, and one well-equipped production studio; transmitting its signal to ten classrooms in one school building; and using twenty receivers (for multiple viewing in certain rooms and to assure spare sets if needed), might cost $50,000 without much penny-pinching. Such a system might be manned by a full-time producer-director, a full-time engineer, a part-time secretary, and part-time cameramen, part-time maintenance personnel, part-time artists, and other production aides for as little as $30,000 per year.

---

[5] Nelson, *op. cit.,* pp. 169–71, 187–88.

This sum does not include teachers' salaries, film-rental costs, and other incidental expenses which may be avoided by using students for various semiskilled production tasks. In the matter of labor, minimum union wage rates (so important in budgeting open-circuit educational broadcasting in certain locations) rarely, if ever, enter into a consideration of operating costs in closed-circuit systems, unless union help is preferred to nonunion personnel in certain labor markets (such as big cities).

These latter figures—$50,000 for investment, $25,000 for operating costs—may serve as a starting point from which to estimate the cost of closed-circuit television when used for the transmission of both pictures and sound from a studio to ten classrooms. Costs rise apace as other receiving classrooms are added and more studios are built, or when the signal is transmitted to other school buildings. In closed-circuit transmissions, costs go up as the distance between transmitter and receiver increases. Costs also rise considerably if a school system uses a more expensive type of camera than those upon which these figures are based. It is assumed here that *vidicon* equipment will provide an adequate picture for most closed-circuit needs. Should the more expensive *image-orthicon* cameras be required by, say, a medical or dental school for high-quality definition in picture transmission, the two cameras and allied equipment would cost $20,000 to $40,000 more than the $50,000 projected here.

Financing For the Future

As we have seen, the history of both open- and closed-circuit television has been intimately bound up, in the matter of finance, with the large foundations—particularly the Ford Foundation. The federal government, through grants and matched-fund programs, has also played a vital role in the growth of educational television. But the future roles of the federal government and the private foundations in the fiscal aspects of educational television remain, at the moment, a matter of conjecture.

From the financial point of view, however, certain factors seem clear. It is estimated that there will be a total of 200 or more educational television stations in operation by 1970, serving the needs of various communities as an educational, nonprofit network and offering classes at all levels of school instruction. Few would dare to estimate the number of closed-circuit installations which will be in operation by then, but experience seems to show that, by and large, closed-circuit instruction can be economically carried on (when compared to the cost of conventional instruction) as long as classes average more than about 200 students. The "economy," of course, also depends on the salaries of those teachers who are freed from their classrooms by television, whether they are replaced, the cost of teaching materials, and many other factors.

All things considered, Nelson and others estimate that, by 1971, the total national investment in open-circuit television will be some $66 million, with operating budgets approaching $34 million a year. Total investment in closed-circuit television is more difficult to estimate, but it will not be much less than $40 million in equipment alone, and the operating budgets of these installations are likely to run to some $20 million each year.

Where is the money going to come from?

Various answers have been given to this question, including such unlikely, but nevertheless sensible, suggestions as a "marriage" between toll or pay television and educational television, the former paying for the latter.[6] Like many another interesting—and even workable—financial scheme for public welfare, this idea does not conform to the ground rules for commercial enterprise in the United States today. Such ideas are unlikely to be attempted, no matter how sensible they sound or how cleverly the plans for them are articulated.

In all likelihood, the future financing of open- and closed-circuit educational television will come from sources already tapped. They will have to be exploited more fruitfully than they are at present, because even today only about *one in ten* educational television stations in operation has a sufficient, sustained source of income. It is a serious matter also that a number of closed-circuit installations, built with a burst of foundation and government largesse, are now unused or only partially used for want of enough capital (or enough fiscal ingenuity) to cover their operation and maintenance costs.

At present, well over half the income of open-circuit stations comes, in one way or another, from tax money via school systems, state, county, or city appropriations. Another fifth is derived from

---

6 Dave Bell, "Making ETV Pay," in the *NAEB Journal* (November-December 1963), 50–53.

private colleges and universities, business and industry, and from civic groups, local foundations, and interested individuals. About one quarter comes from grants made by foundations or other sources for the purpose of carrying out research or experimentation in teaching by television; these are a temporary but frequently vital source of income for many stations.

Some 500 closed-circuit installations were surveyed in 1963 by the National Education Association's Technological Development Project,[7] but their patterns of capitalization and financing are nowhere clarified in the printed report. Lee E. Campion, one of educational television's ablest archivists,[8] indicates that, although local funds and tax money have been instrumental in the growth of closed-circuit television, foundation and private grants and government funds have played much the same role in this area as they have in the financing of broadcast stations. Campion singles out the National Defense Education Act of 1958, though, as one major factor in the tripling of construction of installations in schools and colleges between 1958 and 1962. Government funds granted under the Act were and continue to be of prime importance to the development of closed-circuit television.

Sources. Capitalization of educational television in the future cannot rely on any one or two sources to the degree that it has in the past. One of the reasons for the uncertain fiscal destiny of so many educational television projects, both closed- and open-circuit, is that they were started with one or more temporary sources of funds and the idea that they would shoulder their own burdens of support once they were in operation. Once these initial funds were used up or cut off, many projects found difficulty in finding suitable sources of revenue. Numerous avenues of financial support exist, however, and educational broadcasters are finding and exploiting them with increasing zeal. It remains for these sources to be carefully explored by a large enough number of administrators to insure the future growth of educational broadcasting. Their future importance cannot be anticipated, so they are listed here at random.

1. School systems, universities, and private and public educa-

---

[7] Lee E. Campion and Clarice Y. Kelley, *A Directory of Closed-Circuit Television Installations in American Education with a Pattern of Growth* (Los Angeles and Washington, D.C.: Technological Development Project, National Education Association, Occasional Paper No. 10, 1963), pp. xiv–140.

[8] *Ibid.*, pp. 73–78.

tional institutions of many types may pay directly for open-circuit televised instruction or may use closed-circuit facilities and pay for them out of regular budget appropriations. At present, more than one third of the money spent for televised instruction has come from these sources and, if this instruction continues to be successful, this percentage is likely to increase. Although such financing may not allow for extensive use of television for community-service programs and adult, noncredit education in certain situations, and although these sources may respond erratically to recessions, depressions, public pressure, and the whims of boards of education, college trustees, and the like, its future role in the growth of educational television is assured.

2. Business, industry, and various civic groups and agencies will provide other sources of capitalization. They have played a more significant role in the present development of educational broadcasting (particularly in the construction and equipment of open-circuit educational stations) than many are aware of. It is doubtful that these sources of support—particularly private industry—will continue to have the same significance they have had in the past, but some private capital can be expected for educational broadcasting as long as business continues to thrive in the United States.

3. The public will be called upon to contribute to the construction and operation of educational stations. In certain instances, closed-circuit transmissions will be sponsored in housing projects, civic centers, and the like. Although it has been—and probably will continue to be—difficult to convince people to contribute to educational television (probably because they associate television with free commercial broadcasting), in-school education, college courses, adult education, and professional education may sometimes have enough appeal to motivate contributions. Activation of the public as a significant source of revenue is a difficult challenge; only one educational station seems to have met it successfully thus far.

4. Foundation grants will continue to be given for educational broadcasting of all kinds. These large contributions, however, are most likely to be made henceforth mostly on national or state levels: educational network clearinghouses, state educational television boards, libraries and distributors of educational kinescopes and tapes, and the like. It is doubtful that grants will continue in great number to local stations for the construction and operation

of closed-circuit installations and other smaller projects, except where foundations continue to support educational research in the use of new media on a relatively short-term basis and for highly specific purposes.

5. Funds will also come from production contracts whereby individual stations will record, on film or tape, an individual lesson or a series of lessons which are eventually made available to other stations and closed-circuit systems in the United States or abroad. That some of these programs may even be rented for transmission on commercial outlets is not beyond the realm of possibility, and this distribution may pay for the cost of production and might yield formidable profits for the stations producing them.

6. Of course, the federal government will continue to play an important part, direct or indirect, in the future financing of all types of educational broadcasting. Further legislation of the nature of the National Education Defense Act of 1958 can be anticipated in the future; federal aid to the various states will probably be broadened and widened to cover subsidies to educational institutions (at present locally or privately supported) and some of this money will be used for television. Also, new forms of federal revenue for educational broadcasting may appear: taxes may be levied on commercial broadcasters for their use of the public's air waves, or a direct tax may be levied on television sets (as it is in Great Britain), much as the states tax automobiles by means of registration and licensing.

All these alternatives are possible choices for the future. The costs of educational television are likely to remain high—as high or perhaps even higher than the costs of conventional instruction, despite the original hopes of certain educators that televised education would one day become the great discount supermarket of American education. These administrators based their plans on the savings on teachers' salaries and education resources, a vision relatively realistic in dealing with initial investments.[9] What they underestimated was the high cost of operating an educational station or closed-circuit system under any conditions.

These early enthusiasts recognized one factor about the value of educational television that remains true: no matter what the costs, the nation possesses the material resources to provide effective

9 Alexander J. Stoddard, *Schools for Tomorrow* (New York: Fund for the Advancement of Education, 1957), pp. 31–32, 50–51.

teaching and well-organized and well-presented instruction to all students on all levels. Televised instruction, no matter what its cost and whether or not its primary virtue is that of "economy," is being and will be used to help us reach that goal.

CHAPTER III

Educational Television and
Public-Service Broadcasting

Critics of commercial television frequently bemoan the state of broadcasting in general as it reaches out—and it inevitably must—to capture the large, common-demominator audience. It seems, at present, that this procedure is necessary to keep both managers and stockholders of networks and stations contented.

The expression *vast wasteland,* used by a former chairman of the FCC to describe the current state of commercial television, has become a cliché, invoked by viewers-with-alarm as a call to arms, for the wasteland today is as vast as it was in the early 1960's when it was described.

In reality, there are oases in every desert, and the desert of commercial broadcasting is no exception. Along with a heavy diet of stereotyped foolery, which is never entirely absent from the television screens of any American community, there has also been a share (a lion cub's share, perhaps) of what is known in the trade as *public-service broadcasting,* which includes news broadcasts, documentary features, and programs designed to perform a function for the community. Although these programs are hardly educational in the schoolmaster's sense—that is, they are not part of any formal curriculum on any level of learning—they constitute one aspect of educational television which operates beyond the limits of the classroom and, quite literally, set themselves to the performance of an educational service for whatever public they can muster.

The nearly ninety educational television stations presently in operation in the United States do not, by any means, devote their entire output to instruction. School broadcasting tends to be restricted to the days and hours when school is in session; to fill up the remaining hours with adult education would make for dull programming. Accordingly, these educational stations frequently rely on program material made available to them by the National Educational Television Center, and at least half of NET's library of films and tapes is made up of programs of a general public-service nature rather than of formal instruction.

That public-service broadcasting, on commercial or on educational stations, may indeed constitute the finest form of education is no longer a moot point. For three days after the assassination of President Kennedy, the national television complex provided little *but* such broadcasting, and probably never before in history have so many felt so deeply and so personally the effect of a contemporary event. Other, lesser, examples, such as *Victory At Sea,* the Kefauver crime hearings, and Edward R. Murrow's *See It Now* series come to mind in this regard. The fact is that television, commercial or noncommercial, may reflect education's aims at their highest. As Charles Siepmann wrote in 1964:

> Television is distinctive in its universal reach. No other medium can transport us simultaneously to the scene of action anywhere on earth. . . . Television is distinctive also as a new language, a new art-in-the-making with extraordinary power to quicken the senses and focus the mind on reality.[1]

In short, television can educate everyone to an understanding of what one educational philosopher called *the insistent present.*

Commercial Channels

The concept of public-service broadcasting in the United States has had an interesting history. It reflects both the concept and the execution of public service in government and industry.[2] It is also a history of how a unique relationship among broadcasters, advertisers, the federal government, and its agencies has been worked out. Public-service broadcasting answers a vaguely defined but nonetheless pressing demand that the interest of the public be considered by all broadcasters, commercial and noncommercial alike.

On commercial television channels today, public-service broadcasting represents one phase of serious television service offered

---

1 *The New York Times Magazine* (April 19, 1964), 13.

2 Sidney W. Head, *Broadcasting in America* (Boston: Houghton Mifflin Company, 1956), pp. 361–87.

either locally or via a network.[3] Various stations have responded to the needs of their communities in different ways. Public-service broadcasting has—since 1946, at least, when the FCC issued a document entitled the *Report on Public-Service Responsibility of Broadcast Licensees* (or the "Blue Book")—been generally construed to mean nonentertainment programs: serious discussions of religious, agricultural, and educational (a catchall word) matters. Determination of exactly when these programs were to be presented, and in what proportion to the total number of televised programs, were matters the FCC did not see fit to clear up at that time. Nor has much light been shed on this problem of the ratio of serious programs to entertaining programs on either radio or television in the years since then.

Types of programs. Apart from the semantic haze surrounding the words *public service,* serious, broadly educational programs on commercial channels tend to fall into a number of definite categories, the first of which seems to be of major importance.

Public-service programs may be *sponsored* (paid for by the sale of commercial announcements) or *sustaining* (carried by a network or station out of its own funds). In most big cities, local public-service programs (particularly those that deal with local issues) tend to be sustaining, produced on low budgets but frequently executed with skill and imagination. They are also scheduled at times when they are not likely to conflict with lucrative commercial programs—that is, early in the morning, late in the evening, or on Sundays, when television time is difficult to sell to advertisers.

Commercial public-service programs, however, are another matter. Although they are sometimes broadcast on Sundays or at hours before and after "prime" evening time during the week, their participating advertisers want some assurance of a sizable audience and they are frequently produced with healthy budgets. *Omnibus, Project Twenty, Adventure, See It Now,* and *You Are There* are programs of this type which have since passed into oblivion (as many commercial entertainment shows have as well), but *Twentieth Century, CBS Reports, David Brinkley's News Special, ABC's News Reports* and a host of other "special" documentary shows are, at this writing, still regularly broadcast. So are a number of semi-

---

[3] A. William Bleum, John F. Cox, and Gene McPherson, *Television in the Public Interest* (New York: Hastings House, 1961), pp. 11–21.

serious dramatic programs such as *The Defenders* and *DuPont Show of the Week,* which frequently satisfy adequately the numerous definitions of *public service* which seem acceptable to the FCC.

Far and away the most frequently seen type of public-service program on commercial channels involves news or public affairs and may or may not be sponsored. In the heyday of radio, CBS developed an extensive and skilled staff of correspondents and news analysts and, in the television era, NBC followed suit. ABC, operating on a smaller budget than either of the other two networks, also has some excellent news coverage to its credit. These network operations are usually called to our attention only at time of national elections or world crises, but they are important parts of the public-service function of television.

In addition, both networks and local stations carry promotional and service announcements called *spots,* on behalf of national or community charities, civic organizations, welfare agencies, and the like. Whether or not these spots are educational in any but a superficial sense is open to question, but it has been noted that one network alone devoted in excess of $10 million in commercial time to such announcements, and one station in one medium-sized Midwestern city presented nearly 5800 such "spots" in one three-month period.[4] "Spots" are invariably sustaining—that is, no commercial fee is exacted for their presentation.

The general lack of precision in defining exactly what kind of programs carried on commercial channels is indeed a public service or educational may in itself be a healthy state of affairs, as far as the educational function of commercial stations is concerned. As Bleum, Cox, and McPherson point out, the fact that certain types of program are considered by commercial broadcasters to be public-service programs reveals little about the nature of such programming, but it provides an indication to what commercial broadcasters regard as their responsibilities.

That almost every commercial television station in the country offers such programs (albeit at times unattractive to sponsors) is a clear indication that most broadcasters recognize—in a broad sense, at least—their obligation to contribute in some manner to the education of the public. This may be cold consolation to many armchair critics of present television programming practices, but such

---

[4] Bleum, Cox, and McPherson, *op. cit.,* p. 16.

critics would do well to compare the extent and quality of public-service broadcasting in the United States today to that which obtained during the heyday of radio thirty years ago.

Educational Stations

Few educational stations can afford to originate extensive public-service programming. Rarer still is the educational station which finds it either desirable or necessary to program instruction during both daytime and evening hours—with the exception, of course, of those closed-circuit installations which are used only to broadcast lessons within school systems or universities. Therefore, some sort of television service must fill in these nonteaching hours.

Also, one of the major aims of most of these stations is to provide public-service broadcasts as these have been defined. This programming constitutes one important rationale for the encouragement of these stations by both the government and the large private foundations, for they are supposed to "fill the gap" in broadly educational programming which commercial outlets will not (or cannot, for economic reasons) provide. Accordingly, various systems have been devised for pooling the resources of the educational stations in the United States and elsewhere.

Most important of these is the National Educational Television and Radio Center, with headquarters in New York, offices in Washington, and a distribution center in Ann Arbor, Michigan. NET plays a significant role in distributing instructional as well as public-service programs to educational stations. It also offers, at nominal rates, the cream of educational public-service broadcasting throughout the United States, including all kinds of programs serving a public-service function: public-affairs programs, childrens' programs, discussions of controversial issues, and the like. These programs are recorded on film or on tape. Since as much as ten hours of this material, as well as certain instructional broadcasting, is made available to educational stations each week, it is easy to see how a major share of any station's public-service broadcasting can be filled in with fare provided by NET as well as instruction to schools and nighttime adult education.[5]

---

[5] *Educational Television Directory* (New York: National Educational Television and Radio Center, 1963), pp. 42–46.

Another organization, the National Association of Educational Broadcasters, located in Washington, D.C., and Urbana, Illinois, also distributes taped programs; so do subsidiary agencies of larger organizations, such as the Instructional Television Library project of Cambridge, Massachusetts, New York City, and Lincoln, Nebraska, which offers kinescoped and videotaped instruction on many levels of education as well as various kinds of public-service programs. In fact, as of 1964, more than eighty agencies in the United States, including certain educational television stations with recording facilities and certain private agencies, were offering one or another kind of educational broadcasting materials for rental, at various rates, to noncommercial television stations.[6] In the near future, probably one agency like NET will serve as a clearinghouse for the distribution of all of this material.

Almost every program directory of every open-circuit educational television station in the United States today assumes that the transmission of programs designed to serve the community under the broad heading of *general education* constitutes an obligation to the community which must be fulfilled. This obligation differs from that of commercial broadcasters, for educational broadcasters need not worry about utilizing prime evening hours for these programs at the expense of the profits that might be obtained from commercial shows.

Networks and Program Content

It is likely that present educational television stations in the United States will, within the next decade, be joined by coaxial cable and microwave relay to form a true network, similar to the three which currently carry commercial broadcasts. At that time, it is possible that such organizations as NET and other purveyors of filmed and taped materials for broadcast will curtail their present operations in favor of direct or delayed network programs, broadcast from educational stations across the nation.[7]

How much and what kind of classroom instruction level would be handled by this network and how much programming would be

---

[6] *Instructional Television Materials* (New York: Instructional Television Library Project, 1964), pp. 56–57.

[7] *The Needs of Education for Television Channel Allocations*, Bulletin No. 34017 (Washington, D.C.: USGPO, 1962), pp. x–181.

reserved for local production? These are matters far too involved for guesswork at this time.[8] The various geographical areas of the United States have vastly different educational needs: service which may be adequate for some of the network affiliates may not meet the needs of the others. Many complex problems will have to be solved before this network becomes possible even in theory, much less in practice. The last ten years of educational broadcasting, devoted largely to muscle-flexing and experimentation, have witnessed the rise of state broadcasting systems and other small networks. Probably, therefore, this future network will involve the amalgamation of existing small networks and key educational stations around the country.

It is in the field of public-service broadcasting as a whole, however, that the function of such a network can be considered briefly, even at this time, in view of what public-service broadcasting has and has not accomplished on commercial channels.[9] The areas of programming that will serve educational broadcasters best on a national level[10] are the following:

1. *National news and news analysis,* not necessarily confined to fifteen-minute segments, and occasional special features. These are, at present, broadcast on commercial television, but they could be transmitted daily in detail, with liberal use of filmed and taped segments and would include analyses by partisan observers as well as objective commentaries designed to expand the viewer's understanding of various controversial issues.

2. *Discussion, debates and panels,* on which controversial issues, not matters of common agreement, would be analyzed by proponents of different but legitimate points of view.

3. *The fine arts* should receive a considerable portion of prime evening time each week. Programs would include guided tours through the world's great museums and the presentation of the major dramatic works, operas, and concerts. One facet of the network's concern would be the suitable and liberal dissemination of responsible criticism about the state of art in our culture. These critical programs might even extend to include theater and book reviews.

4. *The lively arts* should be represented—be they seven, as identified

---

8 James Robertson, "A National ETV Network of the Future," in *Proceedings of the Conference on the Economics of Educational Television* (Waltham, Mass.: Brandeis University, 1963), pp. 1–17. Mimeographed.

9 Bleum, Cox, and McPherson, *op. cit.,* pp. 20–21.

10 It is assumed that local needs will be met by local educational and commercial broadcasters.

by Seldes in the 1920's, or seventeen. Films, satirical reviews, jazz, and popular culture in its best contemporary manifestations should be given an intelligent hearing along with articulate and knowing criticism, both positive and negative. Such programming will help to raise the national taste for popular culture somewhere above the present common-denominator level.

5. *Travel and international television* should be a vital part of the service of an educational network. Once the technical problems of instantaneous global television transmission are solved, shows might originate daily from all the world capitals.

6. *The world of the natural and behavioral sciences* should, using whatever dramatic or narrative devices are available, attempt to translate for the normally intelligent, interested viewer the startling progress being made today in physics, chemistry, biology, and allied sciences, as well as recent advances in psychology and sociology. Such programs should attempt primarily to define the role of science in daily life and demonstrate its relationship to modern technology.

7. *Programming for young people* should be of prime importance in the morning (for preschool children), near the dinner hour, and on Sunday evenings. No agenda for such programming need be spelled out here. Suffice it to say that it should serve as an antidote to the drivel (our beloved Captain Kangaroo excepted absolutely) and slambang three-stoogery that our suffering children are "enjoying" at present.

This list could go on for pages, but the examples given are a sufficient indication to what tomorrow's educational television network may be like. Unfortunately, it is much easier to make lists than to make progress.

Criticisms of Public-Service Broadcasting

Criticisms of public-service broadcasting on commercial stations serve little function in a monograph of this size. It is sufficient to say that much of this programming has been good. At times—particularly in periods of deep national concern or world crisis—it has been excellent, providing for the viewer a far more complete picture of the event than any other communications medium. Certain other programs on current issues have effectively combined the newsreel technique developed in the 1930's with the intimate approach of radio's interview techniques.

One other point may be made about general criticism of commercial public-service broadcasting. Many feel that television critics writing for large metropolitan newspapers and for such magazines as *TV Guide* have gone out of their way to be especially kind to the producers and writers of these programs, sometimes with justice— but frequently without. Many noted television critics appear to employ a double standard of evaluation, one for entertainment programs and another for both commercial or sustaining programs of a "serious" nature. This latter standard apparently involves the intention of the broadcaster rather than the quality of the program. The tendency of critics in general, including some of the best, has been to award numerous A's for effort when evaluating public-service programs, primarily because such programs are so infrequently seen on commercial channels.

Critics of public-service broadcasting on educational stations have not been as kind, however, perhaps because "serious" broadcasting does not contrast so sharply with the rest of what is offered on these stations. One recent critic of American television devoted a whole chapter of his book to a broadside against the pedantry of public-service broadcasting.[11] To what end? one wonders. Another, one Eugene Paul, in a colorful book on the carnival world of big-time commercial television, seems to echo the woeful conclusion of many a Madison Avenue sage that educational broadcasting is now and must forever be dull, dull, dull. His case makes up in colorful, superficial evidence what it lacks in vision. He does offer, eventually, the vision of an effective educational-network alternate to the commercial squirrel cage he so adequately describes for nearly three hundred pages.[12]

Gilbert Seldes, one of television's sharpest critics, has done much over the years to encourage excellence on commercial channels. He points to two major errors which have been (and are being) made on educational broadcasters' public-service programs.[13] First, says Seldes, educators have paid too little heed to the razzle-dazzle attention-getting and attention-holding devices characteristic of commercial television. He believes that educators feel that the use of such devices, often irrelevant to the educational content of the program,

---

[11] Yale Roe, *The Television Dilemma* (New York: Hastings House, 1962), pp. 93–107.

[12] Eugene Paul, *The Hungry Eye* (New York: Ballantine Books, Inc., 1962), pp. 267–83.

[13] Gilbert Seldes, "ETV's Community Job," in *Educational Television: The Next Ten Years* (Stanford: The Institution for Communication Research, 1962), pp. 103–17.

corrupt its intellectual quality. Second, he is afraid that educational broadcasters have (or will) merely imitate commercial broadcasters and will suffer by comparison, losing whatever audience they might attract and, in the end, broadcasting nothing but trivia. Although his comments do not apply solely to public-service broadcasts, Seldes' solution to these problems are well worth considering:

> We can overcome them if we think not of how TV is used for one purpose or another, for one seemingly in opposition to another, but as a method, like reading, which can also be used for the most trivial and austere purposes. If we think of people paying attention to it [commercial *and* educational television] in a process which continues as the process of reading continues, not only from early childhood on, but in our daily lives when we in the course of an hour may read a comic strip and road signs and symbols and a book of philosophy—then I believe we need not be too troubled by the dual nature of our instrument.[14]

How neatly Seldes counters the criticism that public-service broadcasting may be (but by no means *must* be) dull on the one hand, or simply a shallow imitation of commercial entertainments on the other! The task of educational broadcasting, he notes, is to accomplish whatever function commercial broadcasters neglect. If they follow Seldes' lead, educational broadcasters will provide public-service programs in considerable quantity and of distinctive quality for many years to come. And they will be contributing to classroom education at all levels.

---

14 *Ibid.*, p. 115.

CHAPTER IV

The Effects of Public-Service Television

The sort of general, informal educational programs described and discussed in Chapter III has been offered since the earliest days of both commercial and educational television. Its prototype was developed in the heyday of radio, and for purposes of television has been heavily salted with visual techniques derived from documentary films and on *The March of Time* (both radio broadcasts and films), and devices developed in film newsreels. In fact, many of them might well be mistaken for one or another serious "short subject" with which motion picture exhibitors padded their programs fifteen or twenty years ago.

Public-service broadcasting has been an integral part of American radio and television for many years. No one can calculate its effects with precision. Critics of broadcasting, nevertheless, have lamented for years that there has not been enough "sustaining time" offered to the public, and therefore a lack of interest by broadcasters what they construe to be the "public interest."

Others—particularly broadcasters—have pointed with justifiable pride to radio's role in selling war bonds during World War II, to television's public-service "spot" announcements for community welfare agencies, and other evidence of broadcasters' awareness of their obligations to the public. They would claim, and *do* claim when they are called before Congress to account for their behavior, that the educational worth of their efforts has been extensive, considering the cumulative aspect of public-service programming over many years.

Broadcasts on Commercial Channels

Do commercial broadcasters care deeply whether or not their public-service offerings actually bear fruit in the minds of their viewers and stimulate them to further study or deeper reflection? Most commercial stations carry either local or network public-service programs so that their coverage of serious topics will satisfy the

FCC's requirements for license renewal every three years. Observers have noted that the number of such serious programs increases at license-renewal time, lest the FCC notice a preponderance of entertainment shows. The impact and effect on viewers are considered, if at all, as secondary matters.

By commercial standards, audiences for public-service broadcasts on commercial stations are small at present. A carefully constructed research volume has drawn the following curious conclusions about the American public's feeling towards serious, informal educational television of all types.[1] First, twice as many people prefer "light" entertainment (comedy, game shows, domestic playlets, and the like) as prefer "heavy" entertainment (serious dramas, ballet, opera, and so on). All except a few almost entirely ignore informational programs of the kind discussed in Chapter III. Even college-educated viewers select such programs a mere 9 per cent of the time when serious programming competes with entertainment; the rest select them only 4 per cent of the time under these conditions.

One must remember that 9 per cent or 4 per cent of the massive television audience is a formidable group of people, but these conclusions are far from an affirmation of the popularity of public-service programming. This study continues:

> What is of particular interest is that the number one suggestion for TV improvement [elicited from the samples studied]—"more information"—that comes mostly and almost unanimously from the educated critics of the medium is not backed up *by them* in *their own* program selections. . . . So the argument that viewers consume so much trivia because trivia fill the schedule is confronted with the hard fact that even the most discriminating choose the trivia more often than not when something else *is* available—especially when that something else is a serious, informative show.[2]

The over-all effects of public-service telecasts, therefore, are likely to be negligible, despite the well-meaning claims concerning their importance to the communities they serve.[3] The reasons appear to run something like this: few people watch public-service educational

---

[1] Gary Steiner, *The People Look at Television* (New York: Alfred A. Knopf, Inc., 1963), pp. 198–204.

[2] *Ibid.*, pp. 202–203. Italics are Steiner's.

[3] A. William Bleum, John F. Cox, and Gene McPherson, *Television in the Public Interest* (New York: Hastings House, 1961), pp. 18–21.

broadcasts on commercial channels because most people prefer light entertainment; light entertainment is therefore given the most professional production, the highest budgets, and the prime time; public-service programs are given low budgets and sloppy production, and presented at odd and inconvenient hours; audiences therefore prefer light entertainment which receives superior production, is programmed at convenient viewing hours and eschew public-service programs—and around we go again. The first cause for this state of affairs is, of course, impossible to locate. Nothing but present practice has ever been attempted.

The fact remains that most public-service programs on commercial stations probably do not affect the thinking of more than a small minority of the viewers served by any television station and they affect the behavior of an even smaller number. The few exceptions are worth noting, however: Americans follow political conventions and election returns with avid interest; occasionally a public figure (e.g., the late Senator Joseph McCarthy) may capture the attention of millions of citizens, who will follow any programs for or against him or his cause; occasional controversial or sentimentally significant programs, such as the *CBS Reports* hour on Mexican migrant workers, ex-President Eisenhower's reminiscences of D-Day, or Mrs. Kennedy's charming tour of the White House, may attract large audiences. Lastly, in times of crisis (the Bay of Pigs Invasion, the Kennedy assassination, or the first space flight by an American) the public seems to demand—and commercial broadcasters appear able and willing to give—public-service broadcast coverage of extremely high quality to the exclusion of almost every other kind of television fare, including commercials.

Broadcasts on Educational Stations

The effects of public-service broadcasting on educational stations are entirely different from those on commercial channels, because both the aims and the methods of operation of the two types of stations are so different. The first questions that must be asked about the audience for educational public-service broadcasts relate to its size and quality.

In 1960, Wilbur Schramm published considerable information about the people who were watching the forty-five noncommercial stations then operating in the United States.[4] There is little reason to believe that the general characteristics of this audience have changed since then, although today about twice as many educational stations are on the air.

First, Schramm found that audiences for educational stations, by the standards used to measure audiences for commercial stations, were small. Out of a potential audience of 25 million viewers (at that time), *only about one person in ten* viewed *any* program on an educational station in a given week in November 1959. There was quite a range in the over-all viewing pattern, however; as many as 72 per cent said they had viewed Pittsburgh's educational Station WQED during the past *month*, and in various other places as many as 20 per cent of the respondents appeared to be regular viewers of some educational stations.

Statistics such as these may be interpreted in many ways and, in summary, Schramm notes that out of this potential audience of well over 20 million viewers, the forty-five stations had a fairly regular audience of at least 8.5 million people. In any one average week they seemed to reach about 2.5 million viewers, which means that these educational stations rarely presented any individual program (which included much direct instruction as well as educational fare in general) which attracted over 5 per cent of the sets in a given community. But, considering the entire available audience for these forty-five stations, about 40 per cent at one time or another viewed these educational stations with sufficient frequency (that is, in excess of once a week) to be called "viewers."

Second, Schramm discovered that, although this audience was small, it was also quite different from the regular television audience because of the following factors: first, viewers of educational stations tended to be more highly educated than nonviewers. Most particularly, individuals who had attended or graduated from college tended to view programs on these stations. Also, in Schramm's words, "educational television was *more* popular, *more* often used, in higher status groups,"[5] where status relates to the socioeconomic position of individuals within their communities. Viewers of educational stations were likely to be members of civic organizations and

---

4 Wilbur Schramm, "The Audiences of Educational Television," in *The Impact of Educational Television* (Urbana, Ill.: University of Illinois Press, 1960), pp. 18–38.
5 *Ibid.*, p. 27. Italics are Schramm's.

to take part in community affairs of various kinds; they were also the sort of people who read books, slick magazines, preferred "highbrow" music, and kept up with public affairs in newspapers. In other words, in matters of education, social class, community participation, and exposure to communication media other than television, the audience for educational broadcasting tended to be an elite. It is also an audience of individuals of influence in their respective communities, who fall into the category called by sociologists *opinion leaders*—people whose judgments are regarded highly by those of lower status. Schramm displays caution, however, in assigning these characteristics to a "typical" viewer, rather than to *all* viewers of educational channels.

Although this audience seems, therefore, to be made up of individuals who need educational television least (a curious paradox relating to the voluntary patronage of most so-called educational material distributed to undifferentiated masses), Schramm conjectures that this audience does not think very highly of educational programs as *television* when comparing them to commercial programs, but values them because of their *educational* value.

Schramm puts this point another way:

> [T]he more personal power an individual has, the more likely he is to be a fan of educational television. . . . Therefore, there is good reason to believe that the educational television audience contains a more-than-usual proportion of influential and opinion leaders [*sic*]. Through them, the educational stations may be distributing . their information and exerting influence far beyond the restricted circle of their viewers.[6]

It is therefore quite probable that, whatever the effects of educational television's public-service programs, they are more extensive in each individual community than the size of the audience would lead one to suspect. This may be particularly relevant when comparing the size of audiences and the possible effects of educational stations with the size of audiences and the possible effects of commercial channels. Numbers alone tell only part of the story in both cases. The questions that must be asked when calculating the effects of any type of television service are: What type of audience is viewing? Why? With what objectives? Different sorts of people tend to watch different kinds of television programs. An audience

---

[6] *Ibid.*, p. 35.

of "opinion leaders" usually exerts an influence in any community out of proportion to the number of viewers in its ranks.

Competition Between Commercial and Educational Stations

In the early 1950's, when over 250 television channels were reserved for educational purposes, enthusiasm ran high for the idea of a fourth network luring viewers away from commercial broadcasting by offering "serious" television. Part of this enthusiasm was concerned with the use of video for direct instruction in schools and at home, but a good measure of it was regarded, as Siepmann has stated, as "a windfall such as education has not received in a hundred years. The world was, in effect, invited to avail itself of the resources of the electronic age.[7]

A full appreciation of this "windfall" included an understanding that formidable audiences would be found for the general educational services of this projected nationwide educational television service. It would become, conjectured many, a large audience like the one found (or cultivated) in Great Britain in the days of radio for the BBC's Home Service, a radio network devoted to broadcasts of a serious and generally educational nature.

Schramm's quoted remarks indicate that such an audience does not seem to be available for educational television in the United States; rather, educational broadcasting seems to attract a minor percentage of the present audiences, and a certain type of viewer hardly typical of the American public at large. Why?

The first answer is that educational broadcasting of every type, even that carried on commercial channels, has to compete with commercial television geared to entertain its audience. That is, educational broadcasts must not only compete with commercial offerings, they must address themselves to audiences long habituated to being amused by the medium of television, and not (with the exception of a few news broadcasts) educated or taught by it in any manner. By analogy, in an amusement park one does not expect a lecture on biochemistry at the end of a roller coaster ride; at a gourmet restaurant, one does not expect the menu to have been prepared by an authority on reducing diets. Most expectations are

---

[7] Charles Siepmann, *TV and Our School Crisis* (New York: Dodd, Mead & Co., 1958), p. 32.

justified by previous experience, and so the television audience is probably more receptive to certain types of entertaining experiences than to educational ones.[8]

Audience resistance to educational television is therefore not unexpected. In the middle 1950's, an interesting study was made in the Boston area. It was based on over 500 interviews, with samples of the population drawn from both high- and low-rental areas, and explored the reasons for which the respondents did *not* view educational broadcasts.[9] The study is of particular significance because Boston was at the time (and is now) served by a VHF educational station, WGBH-TV, one of the pioneer educational television stations in the United States with a reputation for competence in its educational public-service programs.

The criticisms leveled at the educational station were interesting in that two general comments stand out in frequency of response, the first having been elicited from one third of the respondents; the second, from about one fourth. The reason for educational television's lack of popularity was *that people want recreation, relaxation, and entertainment, and educational television does not provide this,* and also *that educational television is dull.*

These two comments require further consideration. Although quite a number of the respondents rarely watched Station WGBH-TV regularly, as many as one fifth were regular viewers, and the majority had exposed themselves at least to some educational television. Most of the viewers seemed to be inclined to judge educational programs in terms of professional commercial broadcasting. For instance, the "amateurism" of the educational broadcasts (a term which might have a number of meanings to the respondents), which demonstrated considerable imagined viewer sophistication with the art of television, was cited by a formidable number of respondents.

Other studies tend to confirm these results.[10] In most communities, educational public-service broadcasts tend to be judged by the same standards as commercial broadcasts. In the case of New

[8] See Lawrence I. Costello and George Gordon, *Teach With Television* (New York: Hastings House, 1961), pp. 24–40, for further discussion of the kinds of experiences television seems able to communicate and those which it does not seem to transmit readily.

[9] Kent Geiger and Robert Sopol, "Educational Television in Boston," in *The Impact of Educational Television, op. cit.,* pp. 39–67.

[10] See Schramm, *op. cit.,* pp. 68–113, for two other essays on audience response to educational programs.

York City, where VHF Channel 13 was put into use in September 1962 as an educational station after years of political infighting as Station WNDT, critics and the general public at first tended to lean over backwards to make positive evaluations of the programs it carried. They sang its praises even when there was little to be enthusiastic about. Soon the honeymoon was over, and much criticism of the kind heard years before in Boston was voiced in New York. It involved judgments of educational broadcasts based on standards fundamentally relevant to commercial light broadcasting.

The tendency to judge all educational broadcasting in this manner has probably been the single factor most responsible for the more-or-less discouraging picture painted by Schramm of the audience for educational television. The public was habituated to commercial broadcasting in America before the introduction of much educational broadcasting, and this early habituation and the expectations aroused by it has probably blunted their appetite for educational programs. This may also explain why educational broadcasting has (it seems) been accepted more readily in foreign countries (Italy and the Soviet Union, among others) than in the United States. Overseas, educational broadcasting has frequently started before or at the same time as light entertainment service and has been received by a public with standards of evaluation less specific and demanding than those of Americans.

Audiences for Educational Broadcasts

Thus, audiences for educational television are relatively small and public-service broadcasting takes an uncomfortable second place in competition with commercial broadcasting. Is there then a positive place for this kind of service today in the United States? Is generally "uplifting," serious broadcasting, by whatever type of station, producing an effect on American life and culture? And is this effect likely to be maintained, increased, or decreased in the future?

James Day, General Manager of educational Station KQED in San Francisco has aptly termed[11] the audience for educational tele-

11 James Day, "Neglected Audiences," in *Proceedings of the Conference on the Economics of Educational Television* (Waltham, Mass.: Brandeis University, 1963), pp. 1–22. Mimeographed.

vision *a neglected audience;* in fact, he sees it as a plurality of neglected audiences. This audience is discouragingly small indeed when compared with the large national audiences mustered for entertaining television programs. It is smaller still when compared to the audiences for special events of a compelling nature, such as the funeral of President Kennedy.

What discourages the public-service broadcaster even more, however, is the audience's general satisfaction with present commercial service, claptrap programming, and even with commercial advertising itself. Not only have a plethora of studies shown that the general audience is quite content with what it gets, but this fact is rubbed into the skin of those who are critical of present service by the almost complete absence of negative criticism on the part of the public through the channels by which public opinion may express itself. Nor is the absence of criticism noticeable only in the society as a whole; one finds it also, with minor exceptions, in educational communities.[12]

Day's "neglected audiences" are, admittedly, small audiences who are not neglected by the medium of television, for they make up a part of the great mass of American viewers. What he sees as neglected are *aspects of interest* in a large part of the great audience. An individual may be satisfied with such light broadcasting as *The Ed Sullivan Show* or *To Tell the Truth.* Neither program is poor television by professional standards, and both are of legitimate interest to a reasonably well-rounded citizen. But there remains a "neglected quality" in such a television viewer that is met by neither show and that might be satisfied by serious broadcasting. Day indicates that this quality may be a keen interest which can be satisfied by any number of different types of educational broadcast: programs designed for special minority groups—ethnic, racial, or religious programs of local or regional interest; programs developing

---

[12] Note that in all of Dr. Conant's books on American education, be they concerned with education in slums, suburbs, or schools of education, the author makes only cursory and brief references to the educational potential of television in the United States. A recent and brilliant book by three outstanding educational philosophers, Harry S. Broudy, B. Othanel Smith, and Joe R. Burnett, *Democracy and Excellence in American Secondary Education* (Chicago: Rand McNally & Co., 1964), manages to weaken its excellence and intellectual consistency by ignoring totally the role of mass media, particularly television, as a device for education in democratic values and the transmission of these values to high school students. So it goes in most of the first-rate educational literature coming off the presses today. In most of it, *television* is not even listed as a topic in the index!

broadly useful recreational skills like folkdancing or photography; programs of "liberal" education outside the classroom setting (e.g., drama or film festivals); or a carefully planned concert series on music, art, literature, or any number of specialized fields. And, of course, such an individual might be expected to be receptive to community-service broadcasts, such as a series on career choices for the young, first aid, or some other socially significant activity.

The fact that an individual may be interested in one or more serious programs of this type in no way precludes the possibility that he may also enjoy *Ben Casey, The Late Late Show* or *The Beverly Hillbillies,* as well. Day makes the essential point, however, that the educational broadcaster must regard his potential viewer as a many-faceted human being, who may be encouraged to meet needs as yet undiscovered and unmet—to become, by means of his viewing experiences, a better man or woman. This development, ideally, should occur in a context of what Day calls *an engagement of the mind,* not in the state of passive reception to which most viewers are habituated by commercial broadcasting. The public-service broadcaster, Day maintains, must show an active concern in helping individuals to develop in hitherto neglected areas of interest and concern.[13]

Wilbur Schramm also makes one essential point about the potential audience for this kind of educational television that deserves to be underscored for every broadcaster who has ever thought of television as an instrument for the informal general education of citizens. It applies particularly in a large, rich, heterogeneous country like the United States, where competition for the attention of mass audiences is carried on with such feverish intensity.

Schramm observes[14] that children in the United States are trained to think of television as entertainment, and to reserve the very notion of education and learning experiences for other facets of their lives. Their attitude toward serious broadcasting, therefore, frequently is negative or derogatory. They are thus discouraged from selecting such broadcasts in favor of those which are more amusing.

The use to which television will be put during the next decades by Americans will depend in part upon the attitudes toward tele-

13 Day, *op. cit.,* pp. 16, 21–22.
14 Wilbur Schramm, "A Note on Children's Use of Television," in *The Impact of Educational Television, op. cit.,* pp. 219–22.

vision learned in school as well as at home. What they ask of the medium will depend on how television has been used as an aid to courses and assignments, on the attitudes engendered by teachers concerning the desirability of self-improvement, on the intelligence level of the individual viewer and the viewing habits of his family, on the number of television experiences open to him at any time, and so forth. Schramm concludes:

> It is a reasonable assumption, however, that the use the child is taught to make of serious television in the elementary school years will largely determine the extent to which he continues to use it through the teens; and if that chance is lost, then the full usefulness of educational television will not become apparent to him, if at all, until he is through school and on his own.[15]

This is the fundamental challenge educational public-service television offers to teachers, administrators, and parents in the United States today.

---

[15] *Ibid.*, p. 222.

CHAPTER V

Instructional Television in the United States

To many, the term *educational television* is confined to the use of the medium for formal classroom instruction. This construction of the term is, of course, incorrect. As we have seen, television of many kinds may be put to the service of education in ways which have nothing to do with formal learning either in the school or at home. The use of television for instructional purposes during the past fifteen years has, however, been one of the most remarkable aspects of the meeting of education and electronics. The story of instructional television and its present applications to American schooling are significant parts of the growth of educational broadcasting.

On Commercial Stations

Some historians of instructional television seem frequently to forget that teaching by television in the United States began on commercial channels. Until the early 1950's, no educational stations were operating in the United States on which instruction by television could be given. By then there were well over a hundred commercial stations in the United States, but it was not until 1953 that Station KUHT, which was licensed for the University of Houston and the Houston public schools, was on the air and offering instruction to Texans, young and old. Commercial broadcasting had been offering regular network service since 1948, however, and instructional broadcasting began on commercial stations at about that time.[1] It is still offered by many of them, particularly by the half-dozen or so commercial outlets around the nation which specialize in educational broadcasting rather than entertainment.

Exactly which station carried which instructional program first is of little importance. What does matter is that millions of viewers had their first experiences with instructional television via a com-

---

[1] Sidney W. Head, *Broadcasting in America* (Boston: Houghton Mifflin Company, 1956), pp. 158, 404.

mercial station, and many of them may continue to associate televised instruction with commercial broadcasting and its drawbacks as an instructional medium (like the early hours at which lessons are broadcast).

One spearhead of instructional broadcasting was probably the educational broadcasts to the Philadelphia public schools begun in 1948 over three commercial stations in that city by Martha Gable and her associates, and continued—with considerable modifications —to the present. These broadcasts, part of an instructional service which includes radio broadcasts as well, have over the years experimented with a wide range of subject-matter materials for students in elementary school classrooms.[2]

In the period before educational stations were being built, one figure emerged whose popularity in educational broadcasting was to extend into a number of telecasts, some more commercial than educational. He was Dr. Frank Baxter, whose dynamic lectures on Shakespeare and his works were carried first by a commercial station in Los Angeles, where his audience numbered 400,000 viewers. Later, his programs were broadcast by numerous other commercial stations throughout America.[3]

From 1948 to 1961, Johns Hopkins' broadly instructional program, *Science Review*, was carried on a national network. And, in the early 1950's, Western Reserve University and New York University started broadcasting credit courses on commercial channels.[4]

The most ambitious instructional series carried by commercial stations is probably the well-known *Continental Classroom*, which began in 1958 and has been carried by the NBC. The program has been taped, kinescoped, and distributed by NBC in cooperation with more than 250 educational organizations, foundations, and other groups. These courses have been offered for credit by various institutions of higher learning throughout the nation. They have attracted large audiences in spite of the fact that they are usually broadcast very early in the morning.[5]

Another college series, presented by New York University and produced and distributed by the Columbia Broadcasting System, is *Sunrise Semester*. Many of the courses in the series have been

---

2 Henry R. Cassirer, *Television Teaching Today* (Paris: UNESCO, 1960), p. 38.
3 *Ibid.,* p. 113 and Head, *op. cit.,* pp. 410–11.
4 Cassirer, *op. cit.,* p. 73.
5 *Ibid.,* pp. 106–113.

broadcast by CBS affiliates, again at usually inconvenient hours (the name of the program tries to make a virtue of this drawback) in various parts of the United States for college credit. Some *Sunrise Semester* teachers, particularly Dr. Floyd Zulli, Jr., the first one, have established national reputations by virtue of their appearances on the series.[6]

All in all, Philip Lewis estimates[7] that 560 school districts and 117 colleges and universities are, at present, using commercial channels for regular instructional purposes. They either purchase time from the commercial outlet or supply the instructional broadcast as a public service to the station which airs it without cost. The use of commercial outlets is, therefore, still a significant part of the picture of instructional broadcasting in America.

On Educational Stations

The extent of the use of the ninety or so noncommercial educational stations for instructional purposes may be estimated from the fact that, when researcher Lawrence E. McKune finished compiling a compendium of televised education today in the United States,[8] he produced a report of nearly 300 pages on the 4743 institutions which had reported on their use of television for instructional purposes. The lion's share of these broadcasts was transmitted over educational television stations.

As originally conceived, these educational stations were designed to provide instruction for students both in school and at home—in addition to fulfilling the broad public-service function treated in preceding chapters. There can be little doubt that they are still fulfilling this function today. A reliable 1961 estimate puts at 250 the number of school systems (elementary and secondary) involved in the great "experiment" of televised instruction. The courses are used by more than 300,000 students in about 7500 schools.[9] Add to this the host of colleges also presently using these facilities and one understands the vital role that instructional television is already playing in education.

---

[6] *Ibid.*, pp. 78–80.

[7] Philip Lewis, *Educational Television Guidebook* (New York: McGraw-Hill Book Company, 1961), p. 26.

[8] Lawrence E. McKune, *National Compendium of Televised Education* (East Lansing, Mich.: Michigan State University, 1963), pp. v–253.

[9] *Teaching by Television* (New York: The Ford Foundation, 1961), p. 1.

Supporters of televised instruction claim numerous advantages for it, citing what they regard as its superiority both to conventional instruction (under certain circumstances) and to closed-circuit instruction. They base their judgments upon observations, and there is much to see because, at present, "practically every course in the school or college curriculum, from first-grade arithmetic to college zoology is being taught somewhere over television."[10]

The strong points of this direct instruction, simply put, are:

1. It is possible to use the best teachers available in a given community—or, on kinescope or tape, in the nation—for televised lessons.
2. One station usually serves a relatively large area (about 8000 square miles, and relay stations extend this distance).
3. Community schools can work together in meeting special needs for their own school systems. In this way, specific gaps in instruction can be filled and the quality of instruction can be remedied.
4. Budgets for community stations are usually larger than for smaller closed-circuit operations. Courses, therefore, can employ more elaborate production techniques, better engineering facilities, more and better visual aids, and so forth.
5. Televised courses can be audited at home, not only by students temporarily or permanently homebound, but also by parents and other members of the community.
6. Community interest rises higher for open-circuit educational broadcasting than for closed-circuit telecasting; sources of support are therefore easier to find.[11]

Uses. Many have been the impressive uses to which educational stations have been put for instruction on all levels of education. Two such uses will be examined, but educators should bear in mind that an indispensable and perhaps major part of the capitalization of these stations was provided by liberal foundation grants. It is unlikely that either of them could have been financed by existing budgets available either to the community or to the institutions involved. The stations were set up by philanthropists as model examples of instructional television and that, in effect, is exactly what they are.

In Alabama, extensive use has been made of open-circuit televised classes on a statewide basis. The purpose of the network of stations was to raise the standard of teaching—some of it pitifully low—throughout the entire state. Although closed-circuit television

---

10 *Ibid.*, p. 4.
11 *Ibid.*, p. 44.

is used to some extent for the distribution of network programs, Alabama's television facility mostly utilizes four television stations in Montgomery, Birmingham, Mumford, and Andalusia. Three of these are VHF stations; the one in Montgomery is on the UHF band, but all school receivers have adapters.

Instruction is broadcast on the elementary and high school level by the Alabama Educational Television Commission in Montgomery. Some 452 high school classes use the four secondary educational courses broadcast daily, and over 12,000 pupils view them in class. On the elementary level, twenty courses are broadcast to 158,000 students in 5502 classrooms.

Some of these classes are offered over the quartet of stations by the Birmingham educational television production unit which concentrates on eleven separate high school subjects. In addition, the University of Alabama broadcasts five extension-division programs, using television to enrich ongoing instruction rather than for direct teaching. Auburn University offers a televised remedial course in English on both credit and noncredit bases. Taken all together, at least 600 schools are making use of instructional open-circuit broadcasting in Alabama. The broadcasts reach a vast number of students, estimated at 300,000 (some, however, have been counted more than once—i.e., each time they view a different instructional program).[12] The actual number of elementary and high school students who use television in their daily schedule of classes is not known.

Most observers seem to agree that instructional television has done in Alabama just exactly what it was intended to do: raise the standard of instruction in the elementary and secondary schools. Use of instructional television on the higher levels of learning appears, thus far to have been limited to augmentative functions. The poor quality of many segregated elementary and secondary schools in the state, and the fact that a television receiver does not care whether the viewer is black or white, are delicate but important points worth raising. With a number of qualifications, they illustrate how instruction by television has been used to ameliorate one community's very special educational shortcomings. The utilization of instructional television's potential to transmit good teaching to

---

[12] McKune, *op. cit.*, pp. 1–4.

an entire state has temporarily arrested, if not solved, many problems peculiar to Alabama's educational system.

Another impressive experiment was undertaken by the Chicago City Junior College which, in 1960, published a detailed final report[13] of its first three years of activity. The report noted that the project, which had been financed by foundation grants, would thereafter be underwritten by the Chicago Board of Education. This point alone indicates that the experimental phase of the project was considered a success.

Here again, the experiment was directly reflective of certain educational problems. The college has six branches, with a common catalog of offerings, serving major areas of the city of Chicago. The institution faced administrative problems, difficulties in matters of duplication and standardization of course material, and similar problems.

In 1956, the institution's *TV College* was begun over an educational open-circuit station, WTTW, on which nine courses were taught each year. The courses were purposely varied during the first three years of the project in order to adhere to the "experimental" nature of the enterprise. They constituted offerings in social science, physical science, literature, biology, English composition, mathematics, modern languages, business, and other typical college courses.

Students were screened and admitted to the program in the usual manner. But, instead of attending classes, they watched telecasts at home and kept up with a prepared study guide designed as an adjunct to the televised lessons. Written assignments were submitted and returned by mail. Conferences, examinations, and other matters related to the courses were handled at a branch of the college, and, at certain appointed hours, questions could be telephoned to an instructor.

During the experimental period, about 5000 students per semester registered for the combined courses, and an added audience of many thousands followed the courses informally. About 65 per cent of the students who enrolled for the television courses finished them and took the final examination.

According to all evaluations made so far, these first years were a

13 Clifford G. Erickson and Hyman M. Chausow, *Chicago's TV College* (Chicago: Chicago City Junior College, August, 1960), pp. iv–98.

raging success. So successful were they, in fact, as to deserve a bit of skepticism. Students who took the televised courses did as well as or better than students who come to conventional classes, when the two groups were equally matched in age and intelligence. The majority of students were women—mostly housewives and other late entrants into the halls of higher learning. During the three-year period, twenty students managed to complete the requirements for the Associate of Arts degree entirely by television. A total of 200 others had received their degrees by doing about half their work in the televised courses.

The evaluators of the experimental phase concluded that junior college courses can be taught as effectively by television as in the classroom, that experimentation with the medium itself proves a healthy stimulant to both students and teachers, that television teaching is not easy, and that the cost per student of television teaching is slightly higher than that for conventional methods of instruction. But the higher cost was outweighed by the generally positive effect which the broadcasts had on the citizens of Chicago, including those who did not register for the courses but merely watched the programs. In particular, the programs seemed to modify their attitudes towards junior colleges in general; in other words, the programs had publicity value as well as educational value.

In both Alabama and Chicago the crucial factor in the operation of the projects was the use of open-circuit television, which reached viewers far from the originating point of the programs. In Alabama, the viewing was done in classrooms, under supervision; in Chicago, more mature students viewed at home but kept up close contact by mail with the institution that provided the instruction. Both projects involved the use of nonprofit educational stations: one UHF and three VHF outlets in Alabama, and one VHF outlet in Chicago. Although the objective of each project was different, both have been successful.

On Closed-Circuit Installations

Closed-circuit television is also a method of transmitting instructional broadcasts with certain distinctive advantages:

1. Closed-circuit television can be employed for simple purposes, such as to magnify a microscopic slide or a demonstration within

a single room or to provide effective communication between two rooms.

2. Closed-circuit installations do not require a license from the FCC (provided signals are not sent through the ether to interfere with other broadcasts), nor are there any regulations in regard to programming.
3. Closed-circuit installations are usually highly flexible, allowing for wide variations in application within a school or school system.
4. Closed-circuit television can be installed in such a manner as to meet the specific requirements of any single school or school system.
5. Closed-circuit television is frequently cheaper to use than open-circuit stations.
6. There is less of a "show business" aura surrounding closed-circuit television than there is in open-circuit broadcasting. In the closed-circuit studio, the business at hand is teaching and little else.

Chapter II noted that closed-circuit installations vary both in nature and in complexity.[14] For certain kinds of television operation, it is even possible to dispense with camera operators by mounting preset cameras, with or without remote-controlled lens turrets which change the angle of focus.

Many of the least elaborate closed-circuit systems use vidicon camera equipment, which is a good deal more rugged than the image-orthicon instruments employed by professional broadcasters much of the time. Also, vidicon cameras may be purchased with as few or as many accessories as are needed in an individual closed-circuit system—that is, with or without mounting bases, a various assortment of lenses, view-finders or remote-control equipment. Closed-circuit broadcasts may also originate from within a conventional classroom, from a specially equipped studio classroom, or from a conventional studio just as elaborate as those used by professional broadcasters.

The program may then be distributed by coaxial cable or low-powered broadcasts to classrooms in the same school building or to a number of buildings within a school system. Cables between buildings may be run underground or on utility poles. Frequently such distribution can be arranged either by a local telephone company or a communications common-carrier distributor. There is also the possibility of using microwave relay facilities but such dis-

---

[14] See Lewis, *op. cit.*, pp. 48–68, where many of these complexities are described in detail and with diagrams.

tribution is expensive and requires permission from the FCC.[15]

Washington County. The best-known and one of the most elaborate closed-circuit facilities in the United States was built under the benevolent patronage of the Ford Foundation in Washington County, Maryland, and started operations in 1956. Educators have come from almost every nation in the world to observe this system in operation. Because so much publicity has been given it elsewhere, the description here will be brief.

The system will eventually link nearly fifty elementary and secondary schools (a total of 20,000 students) by means of about 130 miles of coaxial cable. Programs originate from a building housing five studios and considerable other equipment. As many as six programs may be transmitted simultaneously. The Ford Foundation originally designed the unit to test the Stoddard Plan, an ingenious scheme for economizing on classroom usage and teaching manpower by using televised instruction.[16] At present, according to Robert F. Lesher, coordinator of the project, twenty-five lessons are telecast daily and, integrated with the total school program, make up but a fraction of the total instruction. Elementary telecasts last from fifteen to twenty-five minutes; high school lessons from thirty minutes to a full hour. Various special courses or services, such as advanced mathematics courses, administrative announcements, teachers' meetings, and guidance programs, are also televised.[17]

The experiment has been judged successful by most inspectors (teachers involved, outside experts, researchers, and others). Although the cost of running this system approaches $350,000 per year, it may be met (according to estimates) by the economies outlined in the Stoddard Plan, particularly the savings on teachers' salaries.

One other closed-circuit system which has proved a gold mine for research into the effectiveness of instructional television will be discussed further in Chapter VII. In many ways it is probably a typical use of televised instruction on the college level.

In 1954, with the aid of Ford Foundation funds, Penn State Uni-

---

[15] *Ibid.,* p. 118–21.

[16] Alexander Stoddard, *Schools for Tomorrow* (New York: Fund for the Advancement of Education, 1957) or, for a summary, Lawrence F. Costello and George N. Gordon, *Teach with Television* (New York: Hastings House, 1961), pp. 136–40.

[17] McKune, *op. cit.,* pp. 83–84.

versity began closed-circuit broadcasting to large groups. Cameras were mounted in ordinary classrooms and connected by coaxial cable to other classrooms where matched groups of students viewed the lessons. Other courses were offered to classes by television only, and considerable experimentation was done with "talk-back" systems or devices whereby students in a television classroom could ask the instructor a question. His response would then be relayed back to the originating classroom by wire.

In the words of Ron Slawson, production specialist at Penn State:

> [By 1963] Penn State completed its eighth year of closed-circuit instructional television at the college level. Enrollments in television courses numbered 28,523, viewing in three separate closed-circuit systems on the University Park campus. Up to this time we have telecast a total of ten classes via microwave link to our Altoona Center forty miles from the main campus. Plans for the future include the operation of a fourth closed-circuit system. . . .[18]

Thirty-three courses are currently given over television at Penn State. They include a range of subjects from art to military science (considerable use seems to be made of closed-circuit television by both Army and Air Force Reserve Training Departments). Enrollments in televised courses vary from thirty-five (for archeology) to 1928 (Army).

Obviously, Penn State has found instruction by television to be effective and feasible for a wide range of courses. Utilizing a closed-circuit system originally designed to provide data as to the effectiveness of televised education, the administrators of the university attempted more and more elaborate new uses for television. The original experiments indicated that the use of television in higher education did not seem to reduce the quality of teaching or to lower student accomplishment. They have also demonstrated that once a closed-circuit system has been installed, economies in cost of education per student may be forthcoming if the system is used cleverly.

Production Facilities

Because instructional television may be employed in any number of ways, different production devices may be appropriate for certain broadcasts whether carried over open or closed circuits. Fa-

---

[18] *Ibid.*, 182–83.

cilities which may or may not be needed by all instructional broadcasters, but which are extremely useful for many types of productions, include:

1. *Lenses.* These have already briefly been touched upon, but they are the virtual eye of the television system. Lenses for a 16mm motion picture camera fit vidicon television cameras, and the television lenses vary in size and focal length just as those designed for motion picture cameras. Basically, the three types are *narrow-*, *medium-*, and *wide-angle* lenses, each of which encompasses a progressively wider area. Zoom lenses permit rapid and smooth change of focal length. Changes of lenses on turrets should not be made while a television camera is in operation. Zoom attachments, like revolving lens turrets, may be remote-controlled.

2. *Film chains.* These are devices by which motion pictures (usually on 16mm film) may be televised. A special synchronous projector and camera are used for this purpose. In a simple film chain, a *resolving lens* aligns projector and camera; in more complex systems, a device known as a *multiplexer* allows one to use a two-by-two slide projector or other optical equipment like an opaque (Telop) projection source, filmstrip projectors, a second motion picture projector, and the like.

3. *Film recording devices.* Until a short time ago, these provided the only way in which television programs could be reserved for reuse. They are still useful for transcribing television productions onto celluloid film so that they may be shown on conventional projectors in classrooms. But film recording devices have been largely replaced by tape recorders both in commercial studios and on many educational stations as well. *Kinescoping* is a relatively expensive process because it involves photographing a moving image and recording a sound track as well.

4. *Video tape recorders.* These have become much more popular and useful for recording television broadcasts. Although tape recorders have for years been technically more satisfactory than kinescope devices because they produced a superior reproduced image, until recently their price hovered around the $50,000 mark. The tape itself, similar to sound tape but wider and kept on larger reels, was also expensive. Lately, however, the price of such recording instruments has come down to the $10,000–$15,000 price range. Although the tape is no less expensive than it was before, it may

now be recorded and played back at seven and a half inches per second (as opposed to fifteen inches per second on earlier machines). This means that the tape to record an hour of broadcasting costs about $150.

The main advantage of taped television recordings is that the quality of the picture is indistinguishable from that of a live transmission. At present, a number of manufacturers are working on an even less expensive machine for home and school use which will record both picture and sound on tape of the same width as that now used in sound recordings alone. Models are expected to appear on the market sometime in 1965.

5. *Camera mounts*. These, of various size and types, are essential in all television broadcasting. The camera is mounted on a solid pedestal which may be raised or lowered, and possibly attached to a dollie or wheeled tripod to allow further mobility during a television program. The camera must be so placed as to be able to *pan* (move horizontally) or *tilt* (move vertically), as well as be moved itself into its proper position. (Pans and tilts are accomplished by the camera operator's movement of a pan-tilt handle which changes the direction in which the camera is pointing.)

6. *Lighting*. Television lighting may be simple or complicated, depending upon the type of instruments used and the effects to be achieved. *Light meters* are the devices which indicate whether satisfactory illumination has been achieved for a picture (approximately 250 foot candles for vidicon cameras; 125 for image-orthicon instruments). *Key lighting* is primary-source focused lighting; *back lighting* is illumination from the rear; *fill lighting* is diffused uniform illumination. By combining and balancing these three types of lighting, the television director has control of light, darkness, and shadows and can also create the illusion of depth. Basic types of illuminating equipment are the *scoops* (floodlights), *Fresnel* lights (or a spotlight with a special Fresnel lens), and the *ellipsoid reflector* projection spotlight. Spotlights may usually be fitted with "barn doors" or metal flaps to control the spill of light from the instrument. Television studios are also frequently equipped with various fluorescent lamps which provide a considerably cooler light than the incandescent variety. Lights are usually hung from a grid of pipes mounted on the ceiling of the studio; some of them are installed on a pantograph that can be raised or lowered easily.

Lights are arranged for general flexibility of effects unless exactly the same type of program is to be televised every day.

7. *Audio pick-up equipment.* This includes the wide range of microphones usually seen in a radio studio. Basically, microphones may be unidirectional, bidirectional, and nondirectional, and should be chosen according to the uses to be made of them. The Lavalier microphone (usually unidirectional) is worn around the neck, but microphones may be placed on table- or floorstands as well. A boom microphone (frequently nondirectional) is mounted on wheels and follows the television performer, remaining just beyond camera range. Microphones and audio equipment are also used in the talk-back systems, and the greatest success has been achieved with nondirectional instruments hung overhead. Sound equipment, including microphones and earphones with talk-back mikes, also connects the technical staff of a television production with the director or personnel in the control room.

Message Transmission

Although the transmission of television frequencies is a complex matter, certain basic types of signal dissemination are employed in all television broadcasting on open or closed circuits.

Most open circuits are transmitted over ultra or very high frequencies which are tuned to a definite channel or carrier wave. This wave carries both picture and sound. This is known as RF (Radio Frequency) transmission.

Much the same kind of transmission can be used in a closed-circuit system, but the impulses are not sent through the air; rather, they travel over coaxial cable. By using this RF method of closed-circuit transmission, ordinary television receivers can be used as monitors in a classroom and up to six channels can carry messages at the same time. Sound and picture are transmitted together just as they are in the transmission of commercial broadcasts.

Another method of closed-circuit transmission is *direct video transmission,* which usually provides a picture clearer than that transmitted by RF systems. A coaxial cable carries the picture from camera to receiver, but along no particular channel. In effect, *all* channels are used so that only one picture at a time may be carried by the system. The audio part of the program must be sent over a separate hook-up. The advantage of this system is, of course, the clarity of the picture transmitted, a necessity, when televising a lesson in, say, surgery. Some television installations combine RF and direct video systems: the former is used when many channels are needed or when programs are to be sent over relatively long distances; the latter is reserved for particular broadcasts which require pictures with a high quality of definition.

Coaxial cable itself, the wire so essential for the transmission of television impulses from transmitter to receiver, is a complex of specially insulated copper conductors. It is not the same as conventional wiring for radio or telephone transmissions, although both of these may be sent over coaxial cable (and frequently are when other carriers are not available).

One other type of transmission is the *microwave relay system,* by which a high-frequency channel (not employed for regular broadcasting) is focused into a beam of energy by means of a parabolic reflector. This beam is then transmitted to another such parabolic instrument at a point within the unobstructed line of sight of the first instrument. The television image may thus be sent as far, usually, as the horizon. If it is essential to send the image further, multiple relay stations receive the signal, amplify them, and transmit them to the next instrument along the line.

Microwave relay transmission is not true broadcasting, for its beam cannot be picked up by conventional receivers. But because the signal is transmitted through the atmosphere, federal regulations control the use of microwave systems, both for commercial and for educational purposes.

CHAPTER VI

Instructional Television in Schooling

Describing the role of instructional television in formal schooling is more difficult than might appear at first glance. Even a decade ago, those experimenting with this medium were not exactly sure what sort of animal they had caged. Was television to be used to improve ongoing instruction? to effect economies of personnel and staff? to fill in gaps in incomplete curricula? to free mature students from the inconvenience of attending a university center? to spread wide the influence of a "master teacher"? to provide (in televised pictures, at least) physical facilities that certain school systems might not afford? to relieve some teachers of certain specific burdens in instruction?

All these objectives were relevant to the employment of television in schooling. Television may be brought into formal schooling for any one of a number of reasons—or combinations of them—but only when considered and evaluated in terms of improving present schooling. When the potential use of instructional television is held up to education *as it is,* objectives for televised teaching can be determined. Obviously, if a school of any kind can achieve the best possible instruction and maximum learning without instructional television yet economically, it would be most imprudent for such an institution to consider instructional television. For this reason, "blue-chip" institutions, such as the best private secondary schools, have wisely steered clear of televised courses.[1] Their rejection of televised education seems sensible if the superiority of present courses of study has been clearly established, and if the rejection of television is not simply mulish adherence to tradition. On the other hand, it is quite possible for a single school to use all three forms of instructional television to considerable profit.

---

[1] See J. G. Paltridge, *Educational Television in the Leading Universities of the United States* (Berkeley, Calif.: University of California, 1962), pp. 49–54.

The Uses of Instructional Television

Possibilities for the use of television in instruction on any level appear neatly circumscribed by the question: How should television contribute to learning in a classroom or at home? Terminology has differed, depending on the biases of the authorities,[2] but the matter seems to boil down to three possible types of educational utility for television:

1. Television may be used for *enrichment;* that is, as an added resource, similar to a film, recording, or guest lecture that is supposed to add value to a course of study.

2. Television may be used for *cooperative* or *team teaching,* in which case televised instruction assumes part of the teaching load. The particular role of television in cooperative teaching may vary according to the subject and/or level of education. High school language classes may perform routine drills with televised instruction after a regular lesson from a classroom teacher; college sociology students may hold a question-and-answer period with their regular instructor after viewing a televised lecture by another professor. In any event, the role of television in the teaching-learning process must be clearly defined.

3. Television may be used for *total teaching,* in which no skilled teacher except one appearing on the television screen is involved with the student taking a particular course. Total teaching may be carried on in an elementary school in which the children are supervised by monitors, or it may be conducted for college students in their own homes with the responsibility for "attending" the lesson placed upon the viewer. Total teaching by television becomes less feasible as one moves down from university to high school to elementary school. The question of whether to use television for total

---

[2] Donald G. Tarbet, *Television and Our Schools* (New York: The Ronald Press Company, 1961), p. 13, lists, for instance, five ways in which television may be utilized by schools: (1) enrichment, (2) direct teaching, (3) public relations (a matter peripheral to instruction), (4) in-service education for teachers, and (5) college and adult education uses. The five categories seem to approach the word *utilization* from various angles. On the other hand, Mary Howard Smith, *Using Television in the Classroom* (New York: McGraw-Hill Book Company, Inc., 1961), pp. 15–18, has devised three categories of usage: (1) television as a major resource, (2) television as total instruction, and (3) television as supplementary instruction. The first category seems to cover quite a bit of territory, but arbitrary variations like Tarbet's and Smith's are the rule in the current literature of instructional television.

teaching is also related to the nature of the subject matter, the motivation of the students, the quality of the telecasts, and—most important—the alternative types of instruction that are available.

Most instructional television, whether transmitted over closed or open circuits, seems to fall into one or another of these three categories. There is no reason, however, why a course of study cannot move from one to another category as the nature of subject matter varies or other circumstances change. A college student who finds it difficult to follow a televised course might be advised to switch to a live one; a high school class that has been responding well to an English course might profit from enrichment by television after midterm exams show the extent of its progress and, after the students are habituated to the television receiver in the classroom, the instructor might attempt to carry on cooperative teaching.

To coordinate televised instruction with current school or university programs, it is absolutely necessary that all personnel—administrators, teachers, or monitors—be apprised of the nature of the telecasts and their content in advance. Indifference to this simple fundamental principle of television teaching has probably caused more disillusionment with and hostility toward instructional television than any other factor.

Teaching by Television

Experience shows that there is no single teaching method or technique for television which has appeared to be markedly better than others. Criticisms have been made of instructional broadcasts of many types and it may be wise to consider a summary of these criticisms before moving on to a specific discussion of how teaching by television is carried on.[3]

The first criticism is that most instructional television has closely followed classroom procedure. In certain instances, when a superior teacher achieves his excellence by means of eloquence or rhetorical skill, this imitation is fine. In others, the traditional classroom, replicated for presentation over television, limits the scope and appeal of the lesson. This format precludes the extensive use of different

---

[3] Chester D. Babcock, "Instructional Television and School Curricula," in *Proceedings on the Conference on the Economics of Educational Television* (Waltham, Mass.: Brandeis University, 1963), pp. 14–20.

settings, visual materials, resource people, field trips, and other educational devices which add excitement to teaching. Indeed, the
setting one usually sees on an instructional broadcast is a reproduc-
tion of a classroom, with desk, blackboard, and one or two charts,
maps, or globes. Yet, in reality, both setting and teaching devices in
instructional broadcasting need be limited only by the imagination
of the broadcaster.

Second, instructional broadcasters have been criticized for aping
too closely the techniques of commercial television producers. The
charge shows considerable merit, because educators do tend to
imitate the conventions they have learned from watching commercial television at home. For open-circuit broadcasts, time slots must
be adhered to; hence, it is necessary to plan lessons to begin and
end "on the nose." Directors, floor managers, and even television
teachers (who frequently begin to think of themselves as "performers") find it simple to fall into the behavior patterns of commercial telecasters in the rapid pacing of programs, the use of
unnecessary gimmicks and tricks to attract attention, and an unhealthy focus upon *how* things are done at the expense of *what* is
being said.

Third, the passive nature of the television medium itself—and the
presentational manner of most television teachers—has led many
broadcasters to forget that television has an enormous capacity to
militate against passivity in the viewer. Passivity can be reduced by
simply taking advantage of television's potential to stimulate critical
thinking and problem-solving in the viewer, and by setting this
objective at the outset. There are many ways, according to grade
level and subject matter, in which opposing points of view, evidence
from which the student must draw his own conclusion, and stimuli
for further research and study can be transmitted to students via the
television tube. The tendency to encourage passivity may be one of
the largest problems so far encountered in the experiments with
televised teaching, but it is merely an obstacle, not a dead end.

A fourth problem involved discovering what methods and means
can achieve not only the sense, but also the effect, of *interaction*
among television teachers, classroom teachers, and students. Television aside, an absence of verbal or intellectual interaction between
teachers and students is to be found on all levels of education. It is
true—and sad—that the introduction of television compounds this

problem. But interaction—the give and take of ideas, the posing of and responding to queries, the cross fertilization of ideas—is today a compelling concern *because* it is so vital in the proper use of television. If instructional television serves merely as a device for putting the matter of effective interaction in class into the spotlight of educational thought, it is worth its weight in gold.

Fifth, the emergence of numerous distributing agencies for television courses leads some observers to fear that television may become an agent for decreasing the amount of autonomy local authorities have over what is taught and how. They also worry lest it become a vehicle for greater conformity in the curriculums of schools across the land. That these are possible long-term effects of the extensive use of instructional television there seems little doubt. That such effects are, of themselves, either beneficial or detrimental to education in the United States is a hasty and unwarranted conclusion. Both the problems and their possible solutions need more and closer study. How much local autonomy is needed in schooling? Is conformity to standards of excellence necessarily an evil?

In the light, then, of these frequently heard criticisms of instructional television, what are the vital or most important factors in planning a lesson for video presentation? Quite simply, experience seems to show that they are matters of *ingenuity* and *personality*. Ingenuity means, first, an understanding of the specific strengths of television as a device for communication. For instance, it has a great capacity for focusing on people and props with merciless concentration. It prefers charts and objects wider than they are high because of the aspect ratio of the receiving tube. Like black and white movies, it frequently does not differentiate between different shades of color. It is difficult to show cluttered diagrams or spaces on television. Frequently it is necessary to construct special visual aids peculiarly suitable to the medium. Second, ingenuity also requires taking advantage of the special qualities of television and using them cleverly in teaching. If an old teaching device, taken from classroom procedures, can be employed well on television, it should by all means be used. If it is unsuitable, it should be replaced by something else. If maps need redrawing, they should be redrawn; if scientific experiments need modifying, they should be modified, and so forth.

Personality, on the other hand is a more ephemeral quality, and it is one that television transmits with little distortion. The medium seems to be kinder to low-key personalities, quiet nonbombastic types, but no generalizations apply in all cases. Television has also given blessings to such high-pitched personalities as Milton Berle and Jimmy Durante in the entertainment world, and Dr. Baxter and Leonard Bernstein in their own métiers.

The personality of the television teacher, however, is a matter fundamental to the success of any kind of instructional television. The relationship of this aspect of character to teaching is neatly reflected in Whitehead's often-quoted delineation of a teacher's function, no less apt on the face of a television receiving tube than in front of a classroom:

> The teacher has a double function. It is for him to elicit the enthusiasm by resonance from his own personality, and to provide the environment of a larger knowledge and a firmer purpose. He is there to avoid the waste, which in the lower stages of existence is nature's way of evolution.[4]

This is a job not every one can do. It requires special talents and considerable experience or training.

Television in the Classroom

The various possibilities for transmitting and receiving television signals throughout a school building are numerous, and a detailed study of all the equipment necessary for various systems of signal dissemination are far too complex to examine fully here.[5] One of the simplest uses of television in the classroom is the installation of a commercial receiver or two in the front of the room, with sets of conventional rabbit-ear indoor antennae. If instruction is broadcast over a commercial channel or a VHF educational station, the results may be effective if reception is good. It is also necessary that the teacher using television know exactly what material is to be broadcast and how it fits into the course of study.

Equipment.   If the signal is too weak, outdoor antennae may be needed. Schools may install the same sort of ubiquitous roof-top

---

[4] A. N. Whitehead, *The Aims of Education* (New York: The New American Library, 1953), p. 51.

[5] See the clear but relatively concise descriptions in Philip Lewis, *Educational Television Handbook* (New York: McGraw-Hill Book Company, 1961), pp. 124–56.

metal devices that dot the countryside but, when antennae leads are desired in a number of classrooms, a *splitter* may be used to break up the lead for multiple classroom usage. Master antenna systems of various degrees of complexity may be installed, depending on the strength of the signal, the number of stations to be received (different signals may emanate from different directions), and the number of receivers to be reached.

Many types of receivers are available for classroom reception; choosing the right one is a matter of suiting particular viewing needs. The most serviceable and economical receivers have a twenty-one- to twenty-four-inch viewing surface, which is satisfactory for the average classroom. Matters to be considered in addition to those involved in selecting receivers for home use are: the clarity of the speaker system, the construction of control knobs (set screws are better than friction fits), the ease with which the set may be serviced, the degree to which the construction of the set discourages tampering by students, the addition of safety glass over the tube surface, the amount of glare the receiver picks up, the nature and balance of the stand or cart on which the set will be placed (especially if it is to be mounted with wheels and moved from room to room), and similar matters. A number of manufacturers produce receivers especially modified for school use. These sets are considerably more expensive than home receivers but, in the opinion of many, are well worth the difference in price because of their rugged construction, safety features, and general usefulness in school situations where they are likely to receive rough handling.

Devices also are available which can project a televised image onto a screen with varying degrees of clarity. The larger the projected image, usually, the less the clarity and the greater the need for darkened classrooms. Projectors may be mounted permanently or placed on wheeled carts and taken from room to room as needed. A projector may focus its image from in front of the screen or from behind it; in the latter case, a special translucent screen is necessary. In a large auditorium, it is a good idea to attach the sound system to the public-address unit. All in all, projection devices are relatively expensive, and their use seems most justified when large groups are gathered in school auditoriums. For classroom purposes, direct-viewing instruments are more practical.

In any classroom, discovering the best placement of students and television receivers is largely a matter of trial and error. Usually, it is a good idea to employ two receiving sets, for a ratio of fifteen to twenty students per set is ideal. No more than twenty-five pupils should ever view one twenty-four-inch receiver. The problem of glare can usually be reduced by lowering window blinds or curtains, turning down artificial illumination, and placing the sets against the brightest part of the classroom (usually the windows). A cardboard or plastic visor along the top and sides of the screen may also help to cut down glare.

Multiple sets should be placed so that students have difficulty seeing more than one picture tube at a time. Seats should be placed, usually, in a triangular pattern, with the apex closest to the set. In classrooms with stationary seats, sets must be moved around to find the best places for viewing (which may not necessarily be the front of the room). When television sound is likely to disturb other classes, multiple headphone arrangements can be attached to a single speaker. Many other schemes have been devised for the ingenious placement of receivers in schoolrooms, both for permanent installations and for temporary usage.[6]

School buildings may be modified for instructional television in numerous other ways, depending on the kind and amount of television to be used. Some of the modifications are merely matters of common sense: insuring proper ventilation in television classrooms, providing proper acoustics, installing safety devices for electric wires and plugs, and the like. Others depend upon the specific kind of instructional television being attempted. In closed-circuit operations, one classroom, at least, must usually be converted into a studio. This is generally an expensive process, because floors must be recovered, a control room must be built, and other changes must be made; nevertheless most large classrooms make excellent television studios. Closed-circuit installations also demand space for transmission equipment and storage facilities for props and replacement equipment. In many installations, also, special viewing facilities for administrators and guests are arranged.

The provision of electrical facilities for closed-circuit systems or of current sources for the extensive use of television sometimes presents problems in an old school building. Many schools were built

6 Dave Chapman, *Design for ETV* (New York: Industrial Facilities Laboratories, 1960), contains a number of plans fully illustrated with sketches.

when electrical needs were vastly smaller than they are today. On the other hand, many new schools have been built with an eye toward closed-circuit operations and include closed-circuit conduits of coaxial cable. Most schools can be modified one way or another for closed-circuit distribution, however, and the size and nature of the task depends upon the electrical codes and construction practices in any given community. Main problems center on where and how to run ducts and conduits, where to place fuse boxes and other equipment, where to locate distribution hubs to amplify the signal (which must be placed about every 900 feet), and on the selection of cable thicknesses and power and lighting requirements. Most of these matters are problems for specialists, who know how to provide a maximum of utility and a minimum of hazard. They must also conform with local building codes, and their work is sometimes an expensive undertaking.

For this reason, it is hard to imagine why any new school building of any size should be constructed these days without (1) a master antenna system leading to every classroom, for use with open-circuit television broadcasts; (2) coaxial cable conduits throughout the building for the future installation of closed-circuit television facilities; and (3) sufficient power lines—220 volt lines, if necessary—for the use of television origination equipment *and* enough extra power for tomorrow's electronic equipment, which may include color television transmission, various new sorts of projector devices, electronic teaching machines, television tape recording playbacks, and such.

Using Instructional Television

Just how may television be used in formal education? The answer to this question, of course, depends on the demands made upon the medium: Will it be used for direct instruction? for cooperative teaching? for enrichment? What degree of initiative, maturity, and interest can we expect of the students who will use it? Certain general observations are possible, however, for television—like any other medium of communication—has its thresholds and limits.

One observer commented that much instructional television is mere imitation of classroom teaching. Whether or not such imitation provides the best kind of televised instruction, it is not possible to say; certainly further experimentation with alternatives are welcome. The most popular form of teaching by television, however, is un-questionably the tried-and-true lecture-demonstration method.

The lecture-demonstration method. Commercial television does not usually deal in lecture-demonstrations except briefly during commercials, and even these short messages avoid a straight lecture by the use of clever montages or sequences of visuals. The accent in the most interesting commercials (some, unfortunately, more inter-esting than the programs which follow) is upon demonstration rather than lecture. Words—except for product names and slogans which are repeated *ad nauseam*—are kept to a minimum.

In instructional television, the lecture-demonstration is the most popular method on all levels of education, although its usefulness probably decreases as we move down from college to kindergarten. As in commercial television, the demonstration rather than the lec-ture seems to evoke the greatest interest in viewers.

Demonstrations accompanying the lectures may, of course, in-clude the entire repertoire of audiovisual instruction, including, when possible, material on television tape. Films, filmstrips, slides, phonograph records, and other prepared audiovisual aids may also be used during lectures, as well as maps, charts, and models—either those used for regular classroom instruction or some specially pre-pared by the television teacher and staff for instructional video. So-called *realia*, or actual examples of items discussed in class, may also accompany any lecture and appear on the classroom video screen, transmitted either directly or on film (when it is not practical to bring the object into the television studio). A demonstration of a hive of live hornets is an example of realia most prudently tele-vised on film.

The lecture-demonstration method is, first, quite a test of the powers of a teacher to maintain interest and achieve explanatory clarity. Most lecture-demonstration instructors do not memorize their lectures verbatim; rather, they work from notes and improvise as they do in the classroom. But for most of them television teach-ing seems more demanding than conventional instruction. New ma-terial seems to be used up faster, digressions are less frequent, and the medium appears to direct the viewers' attention toward details rather than toward the general perceptive field, as is the case in the conventional classroom. Discussions of generalities or abstract points are, therefore, frequently difficult on television: lecturers seem most effective when dealing with specifics. Things which can be enumerated, illustrated, or given emphasis tend to be most interesting in televised lessons. Theoretically, however, there is *no* lecture which cannot be televised, and if generalities and abstract matters are handled cleverly by the lecturer there is no reason why they should not be as interesting and as easy to follow as in a regular classroom.

Interviews, panel discussions, and dramatizations. In addition to the lecture-demonstration, other methods of teaching by television are possible. First, interviews with specialists or experts are often rewarding if they are carefully planned, conducted in a natural and relaxed manner, and directly relevant to the concerns of a course of study. Interviews bring fresh faces and new personalities into the televised class and, if they have been clearly articulated to the course of study, are likely to serve as a stimulant for students. The art of interviewing on television is a specialized one, and it is an art which the average television teacher had best learn thoroughly before attempting. Most television teachers have discovered that it takes practice to put a guest at ease in front of the television cameras and encourage him to give of his best and to answer questions directly and to the point.

Panel discussions are risky to attempt with amateurs, but they are likely to be effective devices for the discussion of controversial issues or in attempts to seek out variant points of view relating to matters of taste or opinion. It is well to select a panel that juxtaposes various points of view and personalities. A simple device for providing contrast on panels is to juxtapose the young and the old (or this generation's perspective to the past one's), male and female, and so on.

The number of panelists should be kept to a minimum—never more than four and a moderator—for a host of guests tends to confuse viewers, and makes it impossible to discuss a topic without diversions. The moderator functions best as a referee who introduces the panelists, provides the stimulus of a provocative question when it is needed, and makes sure that all panelists with something to say have a fair chance to say it.

Dramatizations are used in instructional television, by showing films or parts of films relevant to a course of study, by using dramatized material provided by a distributor or kinescopes or television tape, or by employing professional or amateur actors to perform scenes from a play or entire plays. Dramatic performances are frequently difficult undertakings for educational broadcasters. The greatest hazard is that high school and college students tend to judge the dramatizations they see on instructional broadcasts by the same standards they apply to professional productions on commercial television. Because some of the finest professional performers in the nation, as well as highly skilled directors and technicians, are responsible for the commercial fare, amateur efforts usually suffer in comparison—both on technical grounds and in terms of acting talent. Sufficient rehearsal and careful preparation pay off when using dramatic devices in instructional television.

Special uses. Educational stations may employ also on-the-spot transmissions, using mobile transmitters (if they can afford to maintain them) to bring into the classrooms civic occasions, celebrations, conventions, and other ceremonies which may have relevance to one or another course of study. This kind of broadcasting is usually a considerable challenge to the imagination of instructional television personnel. They must justify its expense and trouble when comparing it to a simpler form of broadcasting which might be just as effective.

There is also one important type of instructional television which is almost entirely a demonstration. It is the employment of television to teach a specific skill or a series of skills by showing a competent practitioner at work. Dental schools, for instance, televise proper dental procedures to viewing classrooms because students find the enlarged television picture of the patient's mouth much clearer than any view they might get live in a clinic. The teaching dentist usually explains the procedure as he works, but this kind of explanation can hardly be considered a "lecture" in the usual sense. Surgical skills may also be displayed to medical students in this manner, and color television has been found to be particularly useful when put to this task, for the color of various tissues is frequently an important matter to the surgeon.

Television as a "snooper." Television also has a value as a "snooper" into various situations where the presence of live observers would be a distraction. Sample guidance interviews, for instance, can be televised relatively unobtrusively, and thereafter discussed in detail by a large group of students studying guidance interview techniques. Teachers-in-training can observe other teachers at work without distorting what they see by the effect of their presence. Students who are observed in this manner appear to get used to stationary television equipment very quickly and neophyte teachers accordingly get a clear and undistorted view of a teacher-instructor at work, or an insight into the attempts of one of their own ranks.

Other functions for television as a "snooper" are limited only by the imaginations of those who make it available as a resource. When it is introduced into certain places or covers events that have hitherto remained immune from the prying eyes of still and motion picture cameras, problems in regard to privacy arise. These difficulties, stemming from the fact that a television camera in a stationary position can operate noiselessly and does not distract attention, have been the subject of a number of recent popular books and bring up presently unsolved problems of ethics and law. Certainly, for purposes of instructional television, no one should be televised over open- or closed-circuit television—even if the only part of his anatomy on screen is his upper jaw or left big toe—without his consent and without the knowledge that others are watching. If these conditions are met, few moral problems will be raised by "snooping" with television.

Lastly, mention should be made also of some of the ingenious ways which have been conceived for the dissemination of television signals to schools in areas that are served neither by educational stations nor closed-circuit installations. The most remarkable of these, although numerous wrinkles in operation have yet to be smoothed out, is the Midwest Program of Airborne Television Instruction, Inc. (MPATI), a science-fiction idea come to life. First of all, MPATI recorded, with Ford Foundation funds, a comprehensive series of video-tape lessons in numerous subject-matter areas on the elementary and junior high school level. Then, through the resources of fifteen educational stations in the Midwest, they broadcast to between 1000 and 2000 schools thirty-four courses of study to an estimated 400,000 students in 6500 classrooms.[7] In order to reach schools not served by these stations, however, MPATI has devised a scheme to transmit these programs from an airplane

[7] Lawrence E. McKune, *National Compendium of Televised Education* (East Lansing, Mich.: Michigan State University, 1963), pp. 63–64.

flying over half a dozen Midwestern states. Technical problems thus far have limited this phase of MPATI's operations, but the feasibility of such a method of signal distribution over wide areas has been clearly demonstrated.

Articulation of Instruction

A comment by a noted administrator sums up the major problems in articulating televised instruction to schooling:

> Among the teachers who have tried television teaching, I have found very few who are anxious to give it up, . . . but I know that unless the material is of good quality, the presentation is *appropriate* and *reliable,* and a teacher can count on it *when she expects to,* teachers are not going to turn on the TV set.[8]

A simple matter? One might think so, unless a number of failures in instruction by television are examined in detail. The difference between success and failure is frequently a simple matter. On all levels of education, to whatever purpose television is put, one discovers one fundamental problem involving individuals using it: whether they are students learning Greek history at home, or thirdgraders learning to play the recorder, the central educational issue is the articulation of the lesson to other learning experiences. First, there is the problem of articulation in the subject matter itself, meaning outside readings, museum trips, and term papers (in the case of Greek history) or practice sessions and individual and group instruction (in learning to play the recorder). Secondly, there arises the matter of how the televised lesson is articulated to the student's other educational experiences, his background, his educational objective, the amount and nature of his other studies in the field, the available time at his disposal, and the encouragement he receives. These factors will be crucial in regard to what is often mistakenly described as "the effectiveness of the instructional television." At issue is not the effectiveness of television, but the effectiveness of television *as it relates to other educational problems and how they are solved for individual students.*

Special devices.   Briefly, there are a number of devices that can

---

8 Samuel Brownell "The Administrator's Viewpoint," in Lee S. Dreyfus and Wallace M. Bradley, *Televised Instruction* (Detroit: Wayne State University, 1962), p. 9. Italics added.

help in insuring the utility of instructional television, but they are all subtopics under the all important heading of *careful advance planning* of televised lessons. Here are some of them, variantly useful in solving problems of articulating televised education with school practices for the individual student.

Checksheets are extremely useful for both students and teachers when classroom teachers or students at home do not have ready access to the ears of the television teachers and production staff. They may be mailed or delivered to the staff in charge of the televised lesson and should deal, for cooperating teachers, with problems of clarity of objectives, development of the lesson content, vocabulary, teaching techniques, and so on. They may also ask the classroom teacher—or the student if he is a university student at home—about matters of attention, response, and interest as well as about technical concerns in all cases relating to picture quality, sound, use of visuals, and pacing. Checksheets help television directors and teachers keep up with the reactions of their unseen audiences.

Teachers' guides, issued by the television teacher and staff, are invaluable. They usually indicate the content of each lesson and its objectives and make suggestions for preparatory and follow-up activities, outside readings, and allied devices for the best utilization of televised lessons. These guides may be issued periodically. The advisability of using one printed and bound guide per term or year is a matter for individual decision. Students taking college courses at home usually receive such comprehensive guides to work on and consider them a great convenience. In smaller closed-circuit systems, however, where teachers are likely to vary their teaching methods depending upon the response of students, weekly or daily guides are more practical.

Students' guides for mature or older students may be almost identical to Teachers' guides, minus the professional shorthand or jargon permissible in the latter. Students' guides should indicate assignments, outside activities, and the like and, if total teaching is being attempted, may shoulder the burden of explaining in detail all outside assignments and procedures for checking and correcting them. Homebound students frequently mail assignments to a school or college for correction and individual attention.

There are other feedback devices for television classes, all of which help achieve articulation. In the case of closed-circuit systems, and sometimes in open-circuit operations as well, frequent meetings between the television staff and classroom personnel are helpful. The television teacher's observation of prerecorded lessons may help her improve her teaching. Also, there is much to be said for discussions of the lessons by students, teachers, and the people producing them. The closeness of the studio to the classroom is one of the main advantages of closed-circuit television, of course. On open-circuit systems, or where studio and classroom are physically or psychologically distant, mail from cooperating teachers and students may be solicited and—as in the case of many college courses —even required as assignments.

Inviting telephone calls from students and cooperating teachers is, under suitable circumstances, still another way of achieving a sense of articulation, but there are other tricks of television teaching which the ingenious video teacher may employ. A television teacher might display homemade Christmas cards, read student compositions, invite groups of students to her studio as guests during programs, and so forth. Feedback is a problem of ingenuity in instructional broadcasting, and it has been solved in amusing ways. Occasionally, an instructional television program on an educational station with a relatively small audience can elicit a more lively response than an expensive and popular commercial entertainment program. This paradox is one of the most heartening indications for all educational broadcasting in the future.

One final point may belabor the obvious: all television classes under all circumstances ought to use, within a given curriculum, the same text materials (same editions), and the same or similar classroom exercises. And they should all be evaluated in the same manner. The exception is when television is used merely for enrichment or as an adjunct to individual instruction. Where direct total teaching and cooperative teaching are undertaken, it is usually a good idea to impress upon the minds of all involved (cooperating teachers, classroom monitors, and students) the necessity of doing outside assignments, readings, and follow-up work from as homogeneous a set of educational materials as possible. A little error, like an assignment to solve a series of math problems in an edition of a text paginated differently from the one the television teacher is using, may have distressing consequences and lead to unnecessary

comments about the "impersonality" and "mechanization" of televised education. "This could never have happened twenty years
ago," the old-timer may sigh. The old-timer is right, of course, and
so special care is often needed.

CHAPTER VII

Effectiveness of Instructional Television

The news was expected before it came. When it came it was the object of a good deal of crowing, theorizing, and the like. A good number of detractors claimed the sources from which it emerged were biased, that it was irrelevant to any concern of man on earth, that it was interesting but impractical. This bombshell is by now passing into history, but the educational landscape does not quite look the same as it did before.

Matched-Group Experiments

The news was, simply, that in most cases, under controlled experiments, students taught by television did about as well—sometimes worse, frequently better—as students taught under normal conditions. In other words, there was, for the most part, no appreciable difference noted between live classes and television classes. This piece of iconoclastic information appeared to hold true under an enormously wide range of conditions: whether the subject matter was abstract or concrete, whether the teaching was of concepts or of skills. It held true for students in grade schools, in high schools, in colleges, or in universities. And in most cases it held true whether television was used for enrichment, for cooperative teaching, or— where it could be tested—for total teaching.

Some teachers, discouraged for one or another reason by the news, brought up a number of points, all relevant to recent experimentation with educational television but relevant to much other educational experimentation also. Samples of cold water used to douse the fire brought up

1. The "halo" effect which spurs experimental groups (e.g., television classes) to exceed usual norms because they are taking part in an experiment;
2. The real or imagined biases of some researchers who were "out to prove" the effectiveness of television;

3. The hazy and frequently imprecise methods by which student achievement is conventionally measured and which were used in these experiments;
4. The fact that television probably cut down student interaction with teachers, which is an immeasurable but positive quality of good education;
5. The encouragement of conformity in much mass teaching by television, a factor not identified in matched-group experiments but which might nevertheless be present as a result of television teaching; and
6. The warm personal values which the living teacher transmits to a student and which television can never duplicate no matter what experimental data are mustered in its behalf.

The news remained as part of the record, however. No matter how many or what exceptions were entered, the fact remains that students taught by television in widely different kinds of educational situations did about as well—as accomplishment is measured—as students taught by conventional methods. Although this fact does not close discussion on the issue, the shouts of "foul" have not yet caused any crisis more severe than a re-examination of the evidence, its validation, and the necessity of responsible educators to accept it as a fact of life.

The specific results of most experimentation with instructional television have been boiled down into a number of definitive studies. Three documents contain a detailed analysis of most of the experiments conducted thus far. Test after test verifies, in one way or another, the same results concerning the comparability of instructional television classes with live classroom teaching and learning.[1]

Digest of results. These digests have themselves been digested, and in 1962 Wilbur Schramm took a close and impartial look at the sum total of the research done thus far on the effectiveness of instructional television.[2] To begin with, of 393 comparisons between instructional television and live instruction "in 65 per cent

[1] These three compendia are Hideya Kumata, *An Inventory of Instructional Television Research* (Ann Arbor, Mich.: Educational Television and Radio Center, 1956); Presley D. Holmes, *Television Research in the Teaching-Learner Process* (Detroit: Wayne State University, 1959), and David White Stickell, *Critical Review of the Methodology and Results of Research Comparing Televised and Face-to-face Instruction,* unpublished doctoral thesis, presented at the University of Pennsylvania, University Park, Pennsylvania, 1963.

[2] Wilbur Schramm, "What We Know About Learning from Instructional Television," in *Educational Television: The Next Ten Years* (Stanford: The Institute for Communication Research, 1962), pp. 52–76.

. . . there is no significant difference. In 21 per cent, students learned significantly *more* [by television]; in 14 per cent, they learned significantly less from television."[3]

Grade levels and subject-matter areas. Within this conclusion, however, slight but interesting kinds of differences begin to emerge from the host of data compiled in nearly four hundred detailed studies. First, in Grades 3–9, the greatest proportion of these studies (33 per cent) discovered students to have done better by television instruction than in conventional classes, and the smallest proportion (11 per cent) found they did worse. Accordingly, the proportion of studies showing "no significant difference" was smaller (56 per cent) on the elementary level than on the high school or college level.

For high school students, those studies showing no difference between television and conventional teaching rose to 63 per cent. At the same time, the television groups who excelled dropped to 13 per cent, while those which found television less effective rose to 24 per cent.

The apparent tendency of televised instruction to provide more effective learning in primary grades was markedly confirmed in results from college groups. Here only 3 per cent of the studies cited by Schramm found television more effective; only 13 per cent found it less effective; and 84 per cent showed no significant difference. In other words, although televised instruction was as good as or better than conventional instruction for 89 per cent of the primary groups studied, 76 per cent of the high school groups, and 87 per cent of the college groups, *improvement over conventional teaching by televised instruction* appeared most frequently in the primary groups, less frequently in the high school groups, and least frequently in college and university groups.

There is also a variation in the effectiveness of television teaching according to subject-matter area which was difficult to isolate from the first statistics which had been accumulated. An overview of present data, however, shows that mathematics, science, and social studies have had outstanding success for the groups tested. Language skills, health, and safety education have shown a fair amount of effectiveness on television, while history (as differentiated from

[3] *Ibid.,* p. 53.

social studies), humanities, and literature have had the smallest measure of success. These indices of success have been shown to be irrelevant to grade level, and represent, of course, many different types of instruction both on television and in the classroom.

Results related to which courses at which grade level are likely to be effectively taught via television can also be described. Language skills seem to be least well transmitted by televised instruction on the elementary level; mathematics seems more effectively taught by television in primary grades than in high school. Social studies on television seems to be least well received on the college level, as do the study of the humanities—although common sense might lead us to believe that the humanities are subjects most amenable to television instruction in university courses, since they lend themselves so readily to the lecture-demonstration method of teaching.

Homebound college students, incidentally, seem—on the basis of two fairly small studies—to derive a considerable positive value from televised instruction, and the number who do poorer work at home than at the university is negligible. This result, though, may have little to do with the nature of television courses or the students' reactions to them; it may merely illustrate the maturity and independence of college students.

Learning rate and class size.   As to whether television helps the fast or the slow learner differentially, experimental results are not entirely clear. It has been suggested, however, that in all probability the slow learner and the bright learner profit most from televised teaching because bright students learn rapidly under any circumstances and dull children find that their attention is concentrated for them upon the television screen. Learning from televised classes, like all learning, seems to be a correlate also of the motivation of students, and the ways in which motivation may be stimulated in regular and television classes are numerous. In other words, a class with low motivation to learn will probably learn as little from a live instructor as from instructional television.

There does not seem to be much difference in accomplishment that could be related to class size, no matter what the level. Students, however, prefer small classes. There also exists some evidence that in any research on instructional television, the investigators were (and are) measuring the novelty effect of the medium. But the results of such a number of experiments could hardly have shown so consistently the effectiveness of televised teaching when compared to conventional methods—particularly after a number of years, when the novelty has probably faded.

There remains also the risk that research of the kind reported by Schramm does not measure the important elements of the learning process. If this is so, of course, then conventional methods of measuring student progress are not valid and we have been chasing a phantom for many, many years.

Student-teacher interaction.   Television does indeed, by its nature, seem to cut into student-teacher interaction and even into student-student interaction. It is not certain whether this interaction produces a positive or a negative effect on learning under conventional conditions. But whatever its accomplishment, there is less of it in classes using television. It has been feared that television teaching, being authoritarian in approach, discourages "democratic" behavior in the classroom, but this fear has turned out to be groundless. Television students have also held their own in comparative tests of critical thinking, problem-solving, and other of the sundry incidental virtues of education. They seem to respond favorably to a great variety of different types of televised instruction as well.

In another review of the research to date,[4] Carpenter stresses the fact that experiments have shown that television is useful not only in teaching simple concepts and skills but also in encouraging creativity and stimulating original thinking. He also indicates that television can reinforce previous learning, particularly when it is used with other kinds of instruction involving printed media or classroom teachers.

Factors affecting student learning.   Carpenter brings up corollary questions however, raised by this research on instructional television: Are we testing all students for the right things? What are the qualities which make for differences in quality of instruction, granting that they do not seem to relate to the use of television? Lastly, he notes that, although learning differences between live classes and televised classes may be small, a whole host of practical reasons may militate for or against the use of television in any

[4] C. R. Carpenter, "Review of Research on Instructional Television," in *Proceedings of the Conference on the Economics of Educational Television* (Waltham, Mass.: Brandeis University, 1963), pp. 1–28.

given school situation, and these practical matters merit as much consideration as educational matters. If classrooms are too small for teaching by television, or if scheduling problems stand in its way, these are certainly points which must be taken into account.

Finally, on the basis of current research, he lists the factors which seem to affect positively student learning in instructional television courses of any kind:

1. The quality of sources and resources used;
2. The way in which materials are selected and organized;
3. The surroundings on the television screen in which these materials are presented to viewers;
4. The characteristics of students in terms of aspiration, motivation, abilities, previous training, and state of physical and mental health;
5. The nature of the students' responses to the materials on television;
6. The rewards, penalties, or reinforcements which occur with or during televised instructions;
7. The evaluations and comparisons of achievement rates and performance levels to which the students are subjected.

These are matters which affect education of any kind, but they are particularly relevant to instructional television because the tendency exists for evaluators to blame the medium itself for poor instruction when a series of lessons does not live up to expectations. Frequently, they overlook many other factors which may be involved in both the success and failure of televised instruction.

No eternal truth or hard-and-fast laws of educational methodology are going to emerge from a mere 400 studies of the use of an instrument as flexible as television in a complex as enormous as the school system in the United States. Carpenter admits that some of the students of the research in this field are quite dissatisfied with the rigors (or lack of them) imposed on various experiments. The variable factor being studied in most of them—that is, television—was differently employed from investigation to investigation, or sometimes inconsistently used in certain courses of study, so the factor of television alone was hardly a single variable but, in fact, many variables. Differences of usage at different levels of education for various subjects, the amount of student time spent with television as compared with time spent on other media (books, tape recorders, and so on), and other factors were lost in the shuffle as the numerous studies were lumped together and final conclusions were drawn.

What these still relatively tentative conclusions show about the effectiveness of televised instruction is simply stated. The time has come when television should be given the same serious consideration as a medium of instruction, in and out of schools, as is given to textbooks, workbooks, phonograph records, and—the oldest medium known—the living teacher. As Schramm says:

"The further step we have now taken has put us in position to say something about the conditions under which students learn *more* from television and something about *what* he learns from television."[5] Notice he says we are in a *position* to say something, but a stance is not a swing.

One fair question arises from these studies: Are television classes, by and large, more carefully prepared than live classes? That is, do teachers spend more time preparing them and work harder in teaching them? If so, their general effectiveness is by no means unexpected. Another question may be posed about the values which students receive from the interaction with their teachers: How important, basically, is the student's ability to ask questions of his teacher? Others would ask: Is television just another visual aid, like a film, which is merely easier to introduce into a lesson? Can the talents of superior teachers be extended by television without distortion? How does television help or hinder student concentration? How can television be used to vary the pace of schooling, to provide new faces, new ideas and new stimuli in the conventional classroom?

Questions also arise as to why television seems to add so much more to the educational experiences of a student in the primary grades as opposed to one on the college level. Perhaps this is the result of the manner in which elementary school teachers use television or because small children expect that television will be "fun." Whatever the reasons, they deserve more than theoretical answers.

As many educators have noted, when faced with the fact that instructional television works, frequently in the most unlikely of situations, a good deal more must be known about the whole teaching-learning process in different subjects on all three levels of education before the best theories of how and why instructional television works are worth the paper they are printed on.

---

[5] Schramm, *op. cit.*, p. 66. Italics are Schramm's.

Attitudes Toward Instructional Television

Student attitudes. Learning, of course, is not the only objective of schooling. As much damage to the process of education has probably resulted from hostility on the part of students toward schools and teachers as has come from sinfully outdated textbooks and incompetent Ichabods who help to undermine the cause of decent instruction.

Today, though, so many other factors are involved in the formation of attitudes toward education that nothing like a one-to-one relationship can be said to exist between the effectiveness of any type of teaching and the attitudes of students toward it. If there were such a relationship, some of the most severe educational problems might be easily solved and the art of administration might also be simplified.

The bulk of studies to date, based upon responses from 1203 elementary school children and 2845 high school children who had been exposed to a wide range of different types of instructional television, indicate that younger children believe they learn more from television classes—or at least three quarters of them do. High school students are more skeptical: only about one third believe they get more from televised classes than from conventional instruction. College students, all in all, seem even less enthusiastic than high school students, rating high their preference for live classes over televised instruction under various circumstances and for different kinds of subject matter.

On the other hand, there is quite a bit of evidence that university students who use television at home have generally favorable attitudes toward the instruction. It follows, probably, that general attitudes of college students toward instructional television are probably closely related to what the alternative to television is, or what they think it is.

It is not true that these attitudes are identifiable by age, or school level. As one might expect, these attitudes also reflect how students feel toward teachers and subject matter, as well as toward the medium used. These are subjects (for instance, mathematics) that appear hexed as far as high school students are concerned, and there are teachers whose personalities seem to override antipathy toward any subject.

Students' judgments of individual televised classes and teachers seem to vary widely in almost every group studied. Schramm also notes[6] the evidence, confirmed by these studies but by no means original in them, that a high degree of enjoyment on the part of students correlates highly with the amount learned for any course of study.

College students, from whom one may expect a degree of dispassionate objectivity in regard to their own education, might be expected to show a different pattern of attitudes towards preferred teachers and subjects, but this is not the case. Once again, marked preferences for certain televised courses were noted; antipathies to others were just as apparent. Both seemed to relate, once again, to "favored" subjects and/or "favorite" professors.

There is something of a pattern to these likes and dislikes in regard to instructional television. Courses in which demonstrations are important tend to be favored over courses requiring only discussion and drill. As has been noted, television is particularly hospitable to the lecture-demonstration method. But to assume that subject matter or television alone is the cause of these attitudes carries the use of these studies too far; many other factors are involved in every instance.

The extent to which these attitudes relate to the novelty effect of television, particularly when small children are involved, is another knotty problem that time alone will solve. At Penn State, where instruction by television has been going on for many years, the novelty seems to have worn off and students are judging televised courses today by factors relevant to subject matter and teaching quality. But at Penn State every experiment seems to correlate so strongly with what enthusiasts of televised schooling would presume to be true, that some of their research material demands, in the opinion of some, careful scrutiny beyond the usual safeguards employed in evaluating educational research.[7]

Teacher attitudes. Also crucial to the success or failure of instructional television in the long run are the attitudes of teachers toward it. Traditionally, teachers tend to be conservative, frequently

---

[6] *Ibid.*, p. 57.

[7] L. P. Greenhill and C. R. Carpenter, *An Investigation of Closed-Circuit Television for Teaching University Courses* (University Park, Pa.: Penn State University, 1958).

resistant to change and unimpressed by research in or theories of education. It took a generation for the innovation at Columbia's Teachers College known as *progressive education* to filter, via administrators largely, into the average American classroom. There even remains a large phalanx of "old-fashioned" teachers—some of them young people, curiously enough—who are still resisting the liberal-progressive trend. The rugged, practical business of teaching has been known to reduce any number of theoretical liberals to pragmatic conservatives in a short time.

Such conservatism is also noted in teachers' attitudes toward television, particularly those who fear that television represents a form of technological progress which may cost them their jobs in the long run. When they are finally exposed to television, however, their antipathy does not appear to last long.

It is diminished first among the teachers who actually teach *on* television. They like the medium, the attention it brings them, and the challenges it offers them. Teachers are probably exhibitionists, and television brings out the "ham" in many of them.

Once they get used to it, elementary school teachers seem to enjoy television in their classrooms for cooperative teaching or enrichment. Those who have withstood the strain of teaching on the primary level know that almost any relief from the constant demands of children is welcome, and a well-conceived televised lesson provides a perfect change of pace for young children and teachers.

High school teachers seem more hesitant about accepting televised courses, but as experience with the medium increases, their attitudes tend to become more favorable, especially as they encounter success in using it. As time passes, more high school and elementary school teachers seem to realize that the chances of technological unemployment because of television are slight. A teacher performs so many functions besides teaching, and education itself is so much more elaborate a process than the matter of classroom instruction, that primary and secondary school instructors rightly feel that they will never be replaced by television, or by films, or by any other device short of a perfected robot.

On the college level, however, the picture looks a little different. When television is introduced, faculty members almost invariably tend to take stands of one sort or another against it. Again, at Penn State, faculty attitudes toward instructional television began to become more positive as the medium was used. Teachers who taught on television tended to think highly of it. But for teachers whose sections on the college level are replaced by televised instruction—and on the higher level of education televised courses often replace entire sections of courses—the specter of technological unemployment looms large. These fears may be justified in large measure, for instructional television seems to be able to modify methods of education more drastically at the college level than at lower levels. Individual professors find themselves, even when simple closed-circuit systems are used, facing many times the number of students they used to. As the college population rises, this trend can be expected to increase.

Factors affecting attitudes. Among both students and teachers, instructional television does generate a certain amount of resistance, some of it for good or at least logical reasons; some of it is based on unsound thinking. Only one general maxim may be applied to any resistance to instructional television or, for that matter, to any new method of education or teaching device: *when the amount or quality of what students learn suffers because of an innovation, it is high time to go back to the old way of doing things.*

Much criticism of instructional television does not relate to how much and what is learned, however, and has no basis in what has been discovered in practice. Dale has listed[8] some of the most frequent arguments against instructional television and, with some editorial changes, here they are. Let the reader judge their merits and what may motivate the critics who espouse them:

1. Certain teachers and administrators are chronic rejectors of anything new in education. A change in ways is difficult to take, and the introduction of television is no exception. The argument goes: "Everything works well enough now; why change?"

2. Others accept what they have read or heard about television, but choose conveniently to "forget" it when the time comes to plan improvement in present methods of schooling. Dr. Conant's insistence that only large centralized high schools can save American secondary education is an example of such an argument. Dr. Conant most certainly is aware that instructional television may be introduced to small decentralized high schools, thus avoiding the problems of building and operating

---

[8] Edgar Dale, *The Effects of Television on Teachers and Learners* (Paper delivered at Turkey Run Conference, National Education Association, 1962), pp. 1–24. Mimeographed.

larger schools in certain places. Yet one searches in vain for recognition of this point in Dr. Conant's books on the subject.

3. Some educators say they will "wait and see." What they are waiting for and what they hope to see remains in question. As this book indicates, probably more experimentation has been done on instructional television than on any other device in the history of American schooling. And many innovations—like the creation of the "social studies," the introduction of driver and sex education, instruction in "dating," and new trends in school architecture and classroom design—were in use in thousands of schools (with a paltry backlog of educational research behind them) before anyone decided to "wait and see" anything.

4. Some administrators and teachers are afraid of the administrative reorganizations that instructional television will encourage if devices like the Stoddard Plan are used. The introduction of seminars into high schools, the use of television to encourage creative thinking, the breaking down of neat units and blocks of systematic instruction at the hands of a provocative but unconventional television teacher, are all threats to the security of those who follow present practices.

5. Experiments do not tend to change practices unless the benefits to the learner are clearly visible. In much use of instructional television to date, these benefits have not been made sufficiently clear to teachers, administrators, and students: first, television may heighten motivation because it is new, because it is experimental, and because it relies on modern technology; second, television may be used to clarify difficult ideas and concepts. In Dale's opinion, one of television's major uses is its ability to explain things simply if used artfully and cleverly. Students and teachers using television should be made aware of these advantages.

6. Some teachers worry about being replaced by television. Teachers will not be replaced by any technological device, be it a machine for programmed instruction, a tape recording, or television; rather, the teacher of tomorrow is more likely to be *re-placed*. In Dale's words: "Her tough work begins where the media leave off. Teachers will do what the machines can't do."[9] Even without instructional television, it is likely that the role of the teacher will be modified in the years ahead, what with the trend towards team teaching, the use of teachers' aides, and further specialization of instruction. Television is merely one more factor involved in this modification.

One last important source of resistance to educational and instructional television in the United States is worth considering here, because educators have faced it in the past, will encounter it again and again, and can do little but gird their loins against it.

In America, television grew up in a general environment of commercialism. For this reason, even certain serious students of mass

[9] *Ibid.*, p. 22.

communication in our time label television an "entertainment" medium, sometimes making small concessions to its "informational" value. This description is more or less fair, on the basis of the present operation of the commercial networks. Accordingly, they label print an "informational" medium, films an "entertainment" medium, and radio an "orientation" medium. These are not bad *descriptive* rubrics.

The worst drawback of such labeling is its inaccuracy in the long run and its disregard of potentials. Print can "amuse" or "entertain," movies can "teach," radio can "inform" just as television can do any or all of these things, depending upon who decides what it is to be used for and to what audience it is to be directed. Let us hope this book, if it has done nothing else, has clarified that point.

In employing these facile terms, however, recent students of mass communication have not been propelled by either self-interest or dark motives. On the contrary, they have merely been echoing public opinion concerning what most people have come to expect from these media. As description, this kind of labeling has the value of clarifying functions; for purposes of drawing implications for the future—to use present methods to help create a vision of tomorrow's possibilities—they commit the sin of shortsightedness. Such a perspective tends to keep the status quo where it is.

Public attitudes. Because this bit of what John Kenneth Galbraith calls the "conventional wisdom" is merely a reflection of popular consensus, it is clear where the main centers of resistance to instructional broadcasting do in fact reside. Little attention has been given to this view, but the strongest bastion of resistance to educational broadcasting has probably been the public at large. The very concept of instruction by television runs so strongly counter to what the public has been habituated for more than fifteen years, that much popular support or general encouragement of instructional television cannot be expected.

The sorry conclusion is that the strongest measure of resistance to instructional television comes from the man in the street. He does not express this opinion in the street, but he does make himself heard as a school board member, through his representatives in state and national legislatures, as well as at home when his children tell him that their teacher brought a television set into the classroom. To many Americans, instructional television means today cut-rate education, entertainment pretending to be schooling, time-wasting in the halls of ivy, and the dilution of education.

Studies proving the effectiveness of instructional television on various levels of schooling have little, if any, effect on this larger situation. If, however, the public were given more and better demonstrations of the power and effectiveness of instructional broadcasting both on commercial and on educational channels, if the instruction presently broadcast on the channels were of a higher quality and presented at hours when more of the potential general audience might see it—and if commercial broadcasters at large assumed more of a burden in dignifying the public "image" of television service in the United States—the picture might change. This most formidable source of resistance might vanish.

CHAPTER VIII

The Future of Instructional Television

One morning's mail brought a letter postmarked Bogota, Colombia, and contained a clipping from the June 1964 *Peace Corps Volunteer,* a little pamphlet printed in Washington and sent to members of the Peace Corps and citizens interested in its activities.

The return address indicated that it was from an ex-student of instructional television at New York University whose address is now *Televisora Nacional-ETV,* Bogota, Colombia. A little typed note with it said, in part, "Enclosed is an article that may be of interest to you and your students. Also to others who may enjoy reading about the first Peace Corps ETV project."

This article tells in some detail how American Peace Corps volunteers are beginning to use instructional television in and around Bogota to bring lessons to 100,000 Colombian primary students in 400 classrooms. It goes on to describe the more than twenty telecasts given each week at various grade levels taught by a Colombian Television teacher (*telemaestro*), each lesson being followed by twenty-five minutes of classroom instruction in the schools. Soon the open-circuit system will carry adult education courses to Colombians, some of them who have never seen television of any kind before. Evidently many observers believe that this project is one of the most successful upon which the Peace Corps has embarked, and ex-Project Director John Winnie is quoted as saying: "With educational television we hope to accomplish in ten years what would take one hundred years by conventional means." Inasmuch as 94 per cent of the country's schools are within reception range of the television signal, there is no reason for the project to fail. So far so good; tomorrow will be better.

Bogota's television project is just one example of how open-circuit instructional television can be used to meet the special needs of a small country. In other nations, closed-circuit systems will be used instead, some as part of American foreign-aid programs, some with local funds and staffs. In other nations, private open-circuit facilities will be used.

One prediction is certain: wherever in the world television systems grow today—and they are springing up almost everywhere on the globe in front of and behind the Iron Curtain—they will be used as much, if not more, for education as for entertainment. In all probability, the only countries that will long maintain television service primarily as an amusement medium will be the United States, England, Japan, Mexico, Canada, and some of the Western European nations. Nations emerging from the darker ages may, at present, enjoy endless reruns of films featuring American cowboys and Indians, but they certainly will have more important things to do with television in the future.

Open-Circuit Television

For the United States, reading the future is more difficult, except that educational television is here to stay. Stay it will; the question is where it will be and what it will do.

There is little doubt that all television broadcasting in America will be shifted—sooner rather than later—to UHF bands. This will increase considerably the possibility for creating new stations and finding new outlets for old ones. By itself, this shift may not provide much of a stimulus for the construction of educational stations. UHF stations are as expensive to construct as are VHF stations, but almost certainly a cable and relay network of educational stations will be in operation by 1975. Until that time large Ford Foundation grants already given the National Educational Television and Radio Center will permit it to operate as a quasi-network by distributing tapes and films. What this means specifically, is that the service provided by educational television stations in the United States, both in instructional broadcasts and in public-service broadcasts, will be relatively homogeneous throughout the country. This applies most particularly in the case of public-service programs. In the long run, we may look forward to an educational network, roughly as nationally oriented in content as NBC, CBS, or ABC.

Financing and operation. Prime questions center on who is going to operate this network, with what funds, and for what objectives. There is also the serious matter, in light of its thirty-year record as a government agency, as to whether the FCC is the proper body to administer the stations that make up this network. As Harold Lasswell has suggested,[1] "There is merit in the consideration of the formation of some sort of independent civic board to set standards of performance and see that they are met." There are other possibilities for control also, depending upon what institutions are most deeply involved in educational broadcasting in America and who uses it most.

This fourth network will by no means be a popular network, but because capitalization for commercial profit is forbidden it, popularity will matter little. Individual stations may cultivate different types of listeners and serve different numbers of people. There is evidence that, intellectually at least, America is not as homogeneous a nation as many once believed, and the service of these stations may confirm this fact.[2] Whatever it does, the fourth network will certainly not "sell soap," nor is it likely to "sell culture." It is more probable that it will perform the more modest service of meeting the various educational needs of citizens more conveniently, more fully, and more cheaply than can be done at present. That this fourth network will open up a golden age of culture is too absurd a proposition to discuss here, although it will probably serve as a theme for conference orators for at least a decade to come.

One other guess—this one, a trifle wild: open-circuit television transmission will probably serve most nobly in the area of (1) college teaching, (2) adult education, (3) the broadcasting of civic issues, (4) public service broadcasting, and (5) "highbrow" broadcasting of drama, opera, and the other arts, rather than for direct in-school teaching on either the secondary or primary level. This prediction is made in the face of current successes of elementary and high school telecourses. Closed-circuit television, however, will shortly become so much cheaper and so much easier to use that school administrators will prefer its flexibility and its decentralization of broadcast control to open-circuit transmission. Exceptions to this trend will occur in sparsely populated areas, economically

[1] Harold Lasswell, "ETV's Community Job," in *Educational Television: The Next Ten Years* (Stanford: The Institute for Communications Research, 1962), p. 10.

[2] See Samuel Stouffer, *Communism, Conformity, and Civil Liberties* (New York: Doubleday & Company, Inc., 1955), for an indication of the range of intellectual orientation in America by geographical region, and so on.

unable to provide trained teachers, and socially or culturally backward.

Competition. It is impossible to foresee other functions that open-circuit stations are likely to fill in the future. In one way or another, they will compete with audiences on commercial channels, just as they do today. Commercial broadcasters have, by and large, encouraged the development of educational stations in the United States: they believe that if educational stations accept the burden of public-service programming, valuable time on commercial outlets need not be devoted to relatively unpopular broadcasting. In other words, educational stations will shoulder the burden of serious broadcasting and pressure will no longer be put on the television industry to provide public-service programs.

The reasoning of commercial television executives appears faulty in this matter. Commercial outlets will continue to attract larger audiences than educational stations. Their facilities and talents for broadcasting will be greater. Pressure will be exerted on commercial television from inside the industry by creative artists who want to try their hands at serious telecasting, and the public pressure will rebel against the monomaniacal concentration on entertainment. These forces will keep commercial stations in the business of providing news broadcasts, public-service features, and some (but small) doses of other kinds of serious service. In addition, it is likely that the FCC will continue to demand its moderate tithe of broadcasting "in the public interest" in return for access to the highly lucrative television channels upon which commercial stations operate. So we may look forward to a general increase in public-service broadcasting in the United States, the greater part of it from educational stations but salted with small yet significant offerings from commercial channels.

Closed-Circuit Television

The future use of closed-circuit television is a different matter entirely. It is difficult to predict anything but a healthy future for closed-circuit installations in the United States, particularly when one takes into account three major factors: (1) the probability that prices for equipment will fall sharply in the next few years; (2) the ease with which closed-circuit television will be installed in old school buildings as well as new ones; and (3) the flexibility of the medium in meeting the challenge of so many different problems in schooling and in solving them with a minimum of fuss.

In primary and secondary schools. In public schools, closed-circuit installations will probably be used in four different ways. At least, these seem to be the major possibilities which experts have identified at present:[3]

1. In a single classroom or a single school;
2. To link two or more schools in a system;
3. In statewide networks;
4. In vocational or technical schools, where television is employed almost entirely to demonstrate skills, rather than for conventional television teaching.

In colleges and universities. There are five possible major uses for closed-circuit television in the field of higher education:

1. It may be used in a single classroom or several classrooms (or buildings) within a single college or university;
2. Two or more colleges may be linked in a state or regional system;
3. Mobile units may be employed for telecasting as on-location studios to extend closed-circuit facilities within an institution or among institutions;
4. Special laboratory and experimental stations may be set up for the study of television itself and electronic communication;
5. Television may be put into service for specific teaching purposes in technical, trade, or professional schools.

The growth of closed-circuit systems in recent years is further proof that this medium is at last finding its level of utilization. Part of this growth was no doubt the result of funds made available by the National Defense Act of 1958, but it has nevertheless been remarkable. From a total of 154 installations operating in 1958, there were about 462 in operation by mid-1962. There are more today. Various experiments—both open- and closed-circuit experiments by the New York State Department of Education, a microwave relay system from four major locations in Texas with connections to eleven colleges and universities, and combinations of systems like those in use for many years at Michigan State University (where broadcast and closed-circuit facilities have also been linked to-

---

[3] Lee E. Campion and Clarice Y. Kelley, *A Directory of Closed-Circuit Television Installations in American Education With a Pattern of Growth* (Washington, D.C.: National Education Association, 1963), p. 14.

gether)—indicate that closed-circuit television remains a gold mine of possibilities for educators who are mindful of electronic teaching devices.[4]

On lower levels of education, despite experiments like that conducted in Washington County, Maryland, there does not seem to be the same degree of present activity in closed-circuit transmission, nor does the future look as bright on these levels as on higher levels. The introduction of equipment cheaper and easier to use than that which is standard today might change this picture considerably. In the last analysis, high schools and elementary schools will use closed-circuit broadcasting in the degree to which they need it, and this need will relate closely to the number of pupils in school and the number of available skilled teachers. These problems have by no means reached their most severe dimensions in the United States as yet. According to most authorities, closed-circuit television's "day in the sun" on primary and secondary levels may come, not as a result of decreasing prices and increasing utility of equipment but, rather, because it will be one of the only ways open to keep the quality of education at its present level, to say nothing of improving it.

The extent of use of closed-circuit television in primary and secondary schools will not be independent of the availability of funds, both state and federal, as well as whatever foundation money finds its way into further experimental projects. Need often helps to stimulate funding, as organizations like the Southern Regional Education Board have discovered. For the Southern states involved, instructional telecasts are almost matters of educational life and death because conventional schooling leaves so much to be desired.

In addition, closed-circuit television seems to be moving in various other directions only marginally related to schooling, but of interest nevertheless. Police departments have begun using closed-circuit television to broadcast police line-ups to stationhouses in large cities; nurses and firemen receive refresher courses in hospitals and firehouses via closed-circuit television; television is also used for surveillance of school buildings. Other clever uses are made of closed-circuit television by military installations and by private industry. These uses may have application to education on various levels, including the distribution of audiovisual materials (most par-

4 *Ibid.*, pp. 76–77.

ticularly films) from a central point in a school building to a class-room which need them at a designated time.

Many team-teaching experiments involving closed-circuit trans-missions have also been successfully attempted. At the Richard Byrd Elementary School in Chicago, a specialist teacher broadcasts over closed-circuit television, and less highly paid personnel take over live instruction. Much of this sort of experimentation involving variations of other methods has been going on in the United States for some years.[5]

Indirect teaching. Evidence is also growing that closed-circuit television will not be used only as a direct teaching instrument. It can be employed to transmit tape recordings of superior programs on commercial stations broadcast after school hours but kept "in the can" for classroom use. Closed-circuit systems can also distrib-ute programs taped at convenient times from educational open-circuit stations anywhere in the country. They can also serve as a convenient conduit for the transmission of any kind of open-circuit broadcast on commercial or educational channels. Doubtless, it is the combination of closed-circuit television with other teaching de-vices—tape recordings, movies, special-event programs, filmstrips, and films—that offers some of the most interesting challenges to educators today. And since closed-circuit systems are held to no rules by the FCC as to broadcasting content, they encourage no end of informal experimentation.

Closed-circuit transmission is an aspect of educational broadcast-ing which, quite literally, is limited in its application only by the degree of inventiveness of those who use it. An important question, in fact, is whether a closed-circuit system, using the most sophisti-cated equipment available today and broadcasting in color, is not the ultimate communication device for application in schools.

This question is impossible to answer if one remembers that there was a time when the textbook was considered the ultimate in edu-cational devices. Can one conceive, however, of any more ingeni-ously devised schoolroom than one in which every student has a small closed-circuit television screen built into his desk along with tape-recording equipment and a teaching machine with programmed instruction of various kinds for employment when such material is

[5] *Ibid.,* pp. 66–69.

needed? Such a "student learning unit" would resemble a booth in today's language laboratory, with the addition of a television screen and provision for programmed instruction. Units of this kind might be controlled from a console in the front of the room behind which a teacher might speak with any student without disturbing others at work, or might address the entire class by a public-address system.

Two points must be considered here. First, there is a doubt that any model classroom will ever contain the exact units described above, for any audiovisual device (including television) presently in use may be replaced by a more useful, cheaper item which accomplishes the same ends. For instance, one electronic supply company manufactures at present an 8mm magnetic sound film projector which accepts a preloaded film cartridge and immediately produces a clear sound color motion picture by rear projection. There is no film to touch, to wind or rewind, and no warm-up time is necessary. In slides the cartridge, and the film begins. The instrument is at present quite expensive, but no one can anticipate which audiovisual devices (if any) such an instrument may replace if it can be produced cheaply and if film cartridges can be distributed inexpensively and widely. When it comes to gadgetry, there seems virtually no limit to American ingenuity, and it is not possible to anticipate how this ingenuity will be used in tomorrow's mass media.

Second, and more important, there are many who feel that considerations of uses of multiple electronic and mechanical devices in education constitutes an invitation to conformity, a foretaste of a "brave new world" in education. They see it as a trend toward impersonality, the death of instruction by living teachers, and a move in the direction of a world where "Big Brother" is watching us day and night. Their trepidations are just and merit discussion.

Those who have actually used electronic and mechanical devices in class know well that such fears are not warranted. Gadgets can no more replace teachers or render teacher-pupil contact obsolete than the introduction of the textbook did. Films, slides, teaching machines, and, naturally, television have a place in modern education on all levels. That place varies from subject to subject, from school to school, and probably even from pupil to pupil. Certain kinds of subject matter on certain levels lend themselves best to explanation by film or television; certain rote exercises and drills are best left to live instructors. Students with certain intelligence levels seem to respond well to programmed instruction and the like; others do not.

One of the main tasks facing educational psychologists and philosophers is to spell out exactly which combinations of which kinds of instructions for which pupils will produce optimum results in learning. And let us not confuse the *best* results with the fastest results. Rapid teaching may have its advantages, and the challenge of teaching calculus to fourth-graders may be intriguing, but considering that we have about twelve years to usher our youngsters through their primary and secondary educations and another four to civilize them in college, the question that may fairly be asked of those who would accelerate education is: What's the big hurry? We may do well to slow down a bit and concentrate on better teaching and on deepening and broadening the present quality of learning in our schools.

It is our opinion that those who are looking for the seeds of a George Orwell-type of social order, or who fear that 1984 is already here, have better places than our schools to look to. Let them ponder Vance Packard's concerns in *The Naked Society*[6]—and valid concerns they are—and study the device by which our telephones may be tapped and private lives be invaded. Let them study the legislative legacy which permits snoopers to snoop,[7] rather than take pot shots at educational devices like closed-circuit television or prerecorded courses of study for language labs. These instruments do not aim at brainwashing or thought control, whatever these words connote. They are simply modern media for education. They are as potentially as dangerous or beneficent as a textbook or a map, and, like a textbook or a map, they may be effective or ineffective, well or badly conceived and executed. They may be important liberating forces which play a part in building the good life for the scholars who use them, or instruments of the devil himself. It all depends on how they are used and on who uses them.

---

[6] Vance Packard, *The Naked Society* (New York: David McKay Co., Inc., 1964).

[7] See Morris L. Ernst and Alan U. Schwartz, *Privacy: The Right to Be Let Alone* (New York: The Macmillan Company, 1962).

Bibliography

Campion, Lee E., and Clarice Y. Kelley, *A Directory of Closed-Circuit Television in American Education with a Pattern of Growth*. Washington, D.C.: National Education Association, 1963.

Cassirer, Henry H., *Television Teaching Today*. Paris: UNESCO, 1961.

Costello, Lawrence F., and George N. Gordon, *Teach with Television*. New York: Hastings House, 2nd ed., 1965.

Cross, A. J. Foy, and Irene Cypher, *Audio Visual Education*. New York: Thomas Y. Crowell Company, 1961.

Educational Television: The Next Ten Years. Stanford: The Institute for Communications Research, 1962.

Lewis, Philip, *Educational Television Guidebook*. New York: McGraw-Hill Book Company, 1961.

McKune, Lawrence, *National Compendium of Televised Education*. East Lansing, Mich.: Michigan State University, 1963.

Powell, John Walker, *Channels of Learning*. Washington, D.C.: Public Affairs Press, 1962.

Schramm, Wilbur, *The Impact of Educational Television*. Urbana, Ill.: University of Illinois Press, 1960.

Shayon, Robert Lewis (ed.), *The Eighth Art*. New York: Holt, Rinehart & Winston, Inc., 1962.

Siepmann, Charles A., *TV and Our School Crisis*. New York: Dodd, Mead & Co., 1958.

Smith, Mary Howard, *Using Television in the Classroom*. New York: McGraw-Hill Book Company, 1961.

Stoddard, Alexander, *Schools for Tomorrow: An Educator's Blueprint*. New York: Fund for the Advancement of Education, 1957.

Tarbet, Donald G., *Television and Our Schools*. New York: The Ronald Press Company, 1961.

Index

A

ABC, 32, 98
ABC's News Reports, 31
Adventure, 31
African nations, 15
Alabama Educational Television Commission, 55
Andalusia, Alabama, 55
Ann Arbor, Michigan, 33
Audiences (*see* Public-service broadcasting)
Audio pick-up equipment, 63

B

Babcock, Chester D., 67
Baxter, Dr. Frank, 52, 70
BBC:
  adult education programs, 6
  early television, 5
  Home Service, 44
  school broadcasts, 6
Bell, Dave, 23
Ben Casey, 48
Berle, Milton, 70
Birmingham, Alabama, 55
Bleum, A. William, 31, 32, 35, 40
Blue Book, 31
Bogota, Colombia, 97
Boston, Massachusetts, 45
Broudy, Harry G., 47
Brownell, Samuel, 78
Burnett, Joe R., 47

C

Cambridge, Massachusetts, 34
Camera mounts, 62
Campion, Lee E., 24, 101–103
Canada, 98
Captain Kangaroo, 36
Carpenter, C. R., 87–88, 91
Cassirer, Henry R., 14, 52
CBS, 5, 32, 52, 53, 98
CBS Reports, 31, 41
Chapel Hill, North Carolina, 9
Chapman, Dave, 72
Chausow, Hyman M., 56
Chicago, Illinois, 56–57, 103
Cincinnati, Ohio, 9

Cities using educational television, 9, 14, 33, 34, 42, 45, 46, 52, 55, 56–57
Closed-circuit broadcasting, defined, 3, 13
Coaxial cables, 3, 13, 34, 58, 60, 64, 73
Colleges (*see* Schools and educational television)
Commercial channels:
  competition with educational stations, 44–46, 100
  FCC, 31, 32, 40
  instructional television, 51–53
  public-service broadcasting, 30–33, 37, 39–41
Conant, James B., 47, 93–94
Continental Classroom, 52
Cooperative teaching, 66 (*see also* Team teaching)
Costs:
  open-circuit educational television, 18–20
  closed-circuit educational television, 20–22
  (*see also* Financing sources)
Costello, Lawrence F., 12, 45
Cox, John F., 31, 32, 35, 40

D

D-Day, 41
Dale, Edgar, 93–94
David Brinkley's News Special, 31
Day, James, 46–48
Direct video transmission, 63–64
DuPont Show of the Week, 32
Durante, Jimmy, 70

E

Educational broadcasting, 2
Educational Broadcasting Review, 15
Educational Media Branch of the U.S. Office of Education, 11
Educational stations:
  allocation by FCC, 8
  community, 10
  growth, 9–10
  KQED, 46
  KTHE, 9
  KUHT, 9, 51
  license provisions, 20

Educational stations (*Cont.*)
  NET (*see* NET)
  public-service broadcasting (*see* Public-service broadcasting)
  single agency stations, 10
  state network stations, 10
  WGBH, 45
  WNDT, 46
  WQED, 42
  WTTW, 56
Educational television, defined, 2
Educational Television Directory, 33
Eisenhower, Dwight D., 41
England, 14, 15, 26, 44, 98
Enrichment, 66
Erickson, Clifford G., 56
Ernst, Morris L., 105
Experiments, matched group (*see* Instructional television and formal education, effectiveness)

F

FCC:
  closed-circuit television, 13, 103
  criticism of television by former chairman, 29
  establishment, 4
  license provisions for educational television, 20
  license renewal of commercial channels, 40
  microwave relay facilities, 58–59
  NET, 99
  public-service broadcasting, 31–32, 100
  radio for education hearings, v
  station allocation, 7–8, 10
  UHF signal reception, 3–4
Film chains, 61
Film recording devices, 61
Financing sources:
  closed-circuit educational television, 14
  future sources for educational television:
    business, 25
    civic groups, 25
    educational institutions, 24–25
    federal government, 26
    foundations, 25–26
    production contracts, 26
    public, 25
  open-circuit educational television, 10–13, 23
  (*see also* Costs)

FM, 6–7
Ford Foundation:
  financing closed-circuit educational television, 14, 22
  financing open-circuit educational television, 11–12, 17
  growth of educational television, 11–12
  MPATI, 77
  NET, 17, 98
  Penn State University, 59–60
  Washington County, Maryland, 59
Foreign educational television, 14–16, 26, 44, 46, 98
Foreword, v–viii
France, 15
Free World, 15
Fund for Adult Education, 11
Fund for the Advancement of Education, 11
Future of closed-circuit television, 100–104
  higher education, 101
  indirect teaching uses, 103
  primary and secondary schools, 101–102
Future of open-circuit educational television, 98–100
  areas of operation, 99
  competition with commercial channels, 100
  financing, 99
  operation of network, 99

G

Gable, Martha, 52
Galbraith, John Kenneth, 95
Geiger, Kent, 45
Gould, Jack, 19
Gordon, George N., 12, 45
Greenhill, L. P., 91
Griffiths, Daniel E., ix
Growth of educational television, 7–14
  open-circuit, 7–13
  closed-circuit, 13–14

H

Head, Sidney W., 4, 30, 51
Hennock, Frieda, 8
History of television, 5
Holmes, Presley D., 84
Houston School District, 9
Hull, Richard B., 6

I

Image orthicon instruments, 58
Image of television, 44–45, 95, 104
Instructional television:
  closed-circuit installation, 57–60
    advantages, 57–58
    Penn State University, 59–60
    Stoddard Plan, 59
    Washington County, Maryland, 59
  commercial stations, 51–53
  definition, 2–3
  educational television, difference, 51
  open-circuit educational stations, 53–57
    advantages, 54
    Alabama, 54–56
    Chicago, 56–57
    statistics, 53
  production facilities, 60–63
Instructional television and formal education:
  attitudes, 90–96
    criticism, 93–95
    of public, 95–96
    of students, 90–91
    of teachers, 91–93
  conformity, 69
  effectiveness, 83–89
    class size, 86–87
    factors affecting student learning, 87–88
    grade levels, 85
    homebound students, 86
    interaction between student and teacher, 87
    learning rate, 86
    matched group experiments, 83–84
    subject areas, 85–86
  equipment, 70–73
    antennae, 70–71
    closed-circuit installation, 72–73
    projectors, 71
    ratio of pupils to receivers, 72
    receivers, 71
    splitter, 71
  local autonomy, 69
  methods of teaching, 74–76
    dramatizations, 75–76
    interviews, 75
    lecture demonstrations, 74–75
    panel discussions, 75
    special uses, 76
  objectives, 65
  relating to other educational problems, 78–81

Instructional television and formal education (*Cont.*)
  relating to other educational problems (*Cont.*)
    checksheets, 79
    students' guides, 79
    teachers' guides, 79
  teacher education, 76–77
  teachers, 67–70
    criticism of, 67–69
    ingenuity, 69
    personality, 69–70
  uses, 66–67, 73–77
Instructional Television Library, 34
Interaction in educational television, 68–69
Introduction, 1–2
Iron Curtain, 15, 98
Italy, 15, 46

J

Japan, 98
Joint Council for Educational Television, 11

K

Kefauver crime hearings, 30
Kelley, Clarice Y., 24, 101–103
Kennedy, John F., 5, 30, 41, 47
Kennedy, Mrs. John F., 41
Kinescoping, 61, 75
Kumata, Hideya, 84

L

Lasswell, Harold, 99
Lavalier microphone, 63
Lenses, 58, 61
Lesher, Robert F., 59
Lewis, Philip, 9, 10, 13, 53, 58, 59, 70
Lighting, 62–63
Lincoln, Nebraska, 9, 34
Los Angeles, 52

M

McCarthy, Joseph, 41
McKune, Lawrence E., 53, 55, 59, 77
McPherson, Gene, 31, 32, 35, 40
Madison, Wisconsin, 9
Manford, Alabama, 9
Mechanization in educational television, 104
Message transmission, 63–64
Mexico, 98
Microphones, 63

Microwave relay transmission, 64
Montgomery, Alabama, 55
MPATI, ix, 77–78
Mumford, Alabama, 55
Murrow, Edward R., 30

N

National Association of Broadcasters, v
National Association of Educational
    Broadcasters, 6, 11, 34
National Defense Education Act, 11, 24,
    26, 101
National Education Association's Tech-
    nological Development Project,
    24
NBC, 5, 32, 52, 98
Nelson, Lyle M., 10, 18, 21, 23
NET:
    Educational Television Directory, 33
    Ford Foundation, 17
    function, 10–11
    future:
        areas of operation, 34–36, 99–100
        competition with commercial sta-
            tions, 100
        public-service broadcasting, 30, 33,
            34–36
New York, New York, 33, 34, 46
New York State Department of Educa-
    tion, 101
Nixon, Richard, 5

O

Oedipus Rex, 5–6
Ohio State University's Annual Interna-
    tional Institute for Education by
    Radio, 6
Omnibus, 5–6, 31
Open-circuit broadcasting, defined, 3
Orwell, George, 105

P

Packard, Vance, 105
Paley, Williams S., v
Paltridge, J. G., 65
Passivity in instructional television, 68
Paul, Eugene, 37
Pay television, 23
Peace Corps, 97
Pittsburgh, Pennsylvania, 9, 42
Powell, John Walker, 8, 11
Production facilities (*see* Instructional
    television)
Programmed instruction, 1

Project Twenty, 31
Public-service broadcasting:
    commercial channels, 30–33, 39–41
        audiences, 40–41
        sponsored programs, 31
        spots, 32
        sustained programs, 31
    criticism of, 36–38
    definition, 29
    educational stations, 29–30, 33–36,
        41–49
        audiences, 41–49
        educational network in the future,
            35–36
    effects, 39–49
        commercial channels, 39–41
        educational stations, 41–44
    FCC, 31, 32
    NET, 29–30, 33–34
    program content of future educational
        television network, 35–36
        discussions and debates, 35
        the fine arts, 35
        the lively arts, 35–36
        national news, 35
        natural and behavioral sciences, 36
        programming for young people, 36
        travel and international television,
            36

R

Radio, educational:
    future, 6
    history, 4–5, 6–7
RCA, 5
*Report on Public Service Responsibility
    of Broadcast Licensees*, 31 (*see
    also Blue Book*)
RF transmission, 63–64
Robertson, James, 35
Roe, Yale, 37

S

St. Louis, Missouri, 9
San Francisco, California, 9, 46
School of the Air, 6
Schools and educational television:
    Ames, Iowa, 9
    Auburn University, 55
    Chicago City Junior College, 56
    Columbia, Missouri, 9
    Columbia Teachers' College, 92
    Green Bay, Wisconsin, 9

Schools and educational television (*Cont.*)
Johns Hopkins, 52
Illinois State University, vi
Iowa State, 9
Loyola University, 9
Michigan State, 101
New Orleans, 9
New York University, 52, 97
Notre Dame, 9
Penn State University, 59–60, 91, 92–93
Richard Byrd Elementary School, 103
St. Norbert College, 9
South Bend, Indiana, 9
University of Alabama, 55
University of Houston, 9, 51
University of Missouri, 9
Western Reserve University, 52
Schramm, Wilbur, 41–46, 48, 49, 84–85, 87, 89, 91
Schwartz, Alan U., 105
Science Review, 52
Seattle, Washington, 9
See It Now, 30, 31
Segregated schools, 55–56
Seldes, Gilbert, 37–38
Siepmann, Charles A., 6–7, 10, 30, 44
Skornia, Harry J., v–vii
Slawson, Ron, 60
Smith, B. Othanel, 47
Smith, Mary Howard, 66
"Snooper," 76–77
Sopol, Robert, 45
Southern Regional Education Board, 11, 102
Soviet Union, 14, 15, 46
Statistics of television viewing:
commercial channels, 5–6, 40
educational stations, 42, 53
Steiner, Gary, 40
Stickell, David White, 84
Stoddard, Alexander J., 26, 59
Stoddard Plan, the, 59, 94
Stone, C. Walter, 11
Stouffer, Samuel, 99
Student learning unit, 103–104
Sunrise Semester, ix, 52–53

T

Tarbet, Donald G., 11, 66
Teaching by Television, 53, 54

Teaching and educational television (*see* Instructional television and formal education: methods of teaching, and teachers)
Team teaching, 66, 103
The Beverly Hillbillies, 48
The Defenders, 32
The Ed Sullivan Show, 47
The Late Late Show, 48
The March of Time, 39
The Needs of Education for Television Channel Allocations, 34
Total teaching, 66–67
To Tell the Truth, 47
Town Meeting of the Air, 6
TV Guide, 37
Twentieth Century, 31

U

UHF transmission, 3, 4, 8, 9, 19, 20, 55, 57, 98
UNESCO World Communications, 14
Universities (*see* Schools and educational television)
Urbana, Illinois, 34

V

VHF transmission, 3, 8, 9, 20, 55, 57, 70, 98
Victory at Sea, 30
Video tape recorders, 61–62
Vidicon cameras, 58

W

Washington County, Maryland, ix, 59, 102
Washington, D.C., 34
White House, the, 41
Whitehead, A. N., 1, 70
Winnie, John, 97

Y

You Are There, 31

Z

Zulli, Floyd, Jr., 53
Zworkykin, 5